100 Questions and Answers About Sexual Orientation

Michigan State University
School of Journalism

Front Edge Publishing

For more information and further discussion, visit
news.jrn.msu.edu/culturalcompetence/

Cover art and design by
Rick Nease
www.RickNeaseArt.com

Published by
Front Edge Publishing, LLC
42015 Ford Road, Suite 234
Canton, Michigan

Front Edge Publishing specializes in speed and
flexibility in adapting and updating our books. We
can include links to video and other online media. We
offer discounts on bulk purchases for special events,
corporate training, and small groups. We are able to
customize bulk orders by adding corporate or event
logos on the cover and we can include additional pages
inside describing your event or corporation. For more
information about our fast and flexible publishing or
permission to use our materials, please contact Front
Edge Publishing at info@FrontEdgePublishing.com.

Contents

Acknowledgments

The authors of this guide are Michigan State University students Alexis Stark, Caitlin Taylor and Rebecca Isabelle Fadler. They offered to write this guide after being in a Michigan State University journalism class that created "100 Questions and Answers About Gender Identity."

Alexis Stark, from Farmington, Michigan, studied in the Residential College for the Arts and Humanities, with a minor in women and gender studies. She plans to have a career as a writer. She continued to research and write about gender and sexuality while working for the Center for Poetry and contributing to her honor fraternity, Phi Sigma Pi. Stark is working on a series of children's fairytales that challenge social gender norms.

Caitlin Taylor focused on journalism and women's and gender studies. While working on this guide, Taylor was editor-in-chief of Her Campus at Michigan State University and a reporter for Capital News Service. She previously was a communications intern at MSU's Lesbian, Bisexual, Gay and Transgender Resource Center. Her passion in journalism is elevating women's voices. After graduation, Taylor became an education and courts reporter for The Monroe News in Monroe, Michigan.

Rebecca Isabelle Fadler has two great academic passions: English literature and film studies. In these areas, she engages the world around her simultaneously and in just as much depth as the novels and films she studies. Fadler hopes to continue her education as far as she can, to be happy, to be genuine, and to give back as much as she can. Part of this comes from working as a public relations coordinator at MSU's Resource Center for Persons with Disabilities. That office strives to make campus accessible to people of all perspectives.

We are indebted to several people who advised us or read the guide to help ensure its authenticity and accuracy. That list begins with the people at the Michigan State University LBGT Resource Center, who advised on this guide and one about gender identity from more than a year before work on the guides began. This guide started in a conversation with director **Deanna "Dee" Hurlbert** and was helped by Assistant Director **Alex Lange**, who went on to doctoral studies at the University of Iowa.

Other allies were:

Sarah Blazucki is an at-large board member and former vice president for print and digital media of NLGJA — The Association of LGBTQ Journalists. She also oversees the organization's stylebook committee. Blazucki is communications coordinator at the U.S. Department of Justice's Office of Sex Offender Sentencing, Monitoring, Apprehending, Registering, and Tracking. She previously worked for the U.S. Agency for International Development's Office of Inspector General, the Peace Corps and the Philadelphia Gay News. Thanks to NLGJA Executive Director **Adam Pawlus** for arranging her help on this guide.

Emily Brozovic, graphic and user experience instructional designer at Michigan State University, was one of our advisers and is founder and creator of People Like Me, the first mobile app to find, rate and review LGBTQ+ friendly businesses. You can find the app in Apple's App Store, Google Play and at peoplelikemeapp.com.

Dr. David P. Gushee is Distinguished University Professor of Christian Ethics and director of the Center for Theology and Public Life at Mercer University. Widely regarded as one of the world's leading Christian ethicists, he was elected by his peers to serve as president of the American Academy of Religion and is past president of the Society of Christian Ethics. He is the author, co-author, editor or co-editor of 22 books.

In "Changing Our Mind," published by Read The Spirit Books, Gushee describes his personal and theological journey as he changes his mind about gay, lesbian, bisexual and transgender inclusion in the church.

Susan Horowitz is editor and publisher of Between The Lines/Pride Source. She founded Pride Publishing, Inc., a graphic arts and publishing company and publisher of the New York City Pride Guide from 1983 to 1999. Horowitz was the first executive director of the New Festival, New York's annual gay and lesbian film festival, from 1989 to 1993. She was actively involved in the New York LGBT community in the 1980s and was co-chair and grand marshal of the New York Pride March. She served on the board of the National Gay and Lesbian Task Force in 1983-84 and again in 1993-95. She was a board member of the Seacoast AIDS Resource Center in New Hampshire from 1992 to 1994 and was on the board of Affirmations LGBT Community Center in Ferndale, Michigan.

Eve Kucharski, an editorial assistant at Between The Lines, copy edited this guide. She is a 2017 graduate of Michigan State University with a bachelor's degree in journalism and a concentration in electronic news media. She has been a radio disc jockey and co-host and was an arts and culture editor at City Pulse in Lansing, Michigan.

James Toy is a pioneering civil rights activist who has founded many lesbian and gay rights organizations since coming out on April 15, 1970. In 1972, he co-authored a "Lesbian-Gay Pride Week Proclamation," which the Ann Arbor City Council adopted. Since then, governing bodies across the country have adopted similar measures. Toy also helped the University of Michigan establish and staff an office addressing sexual orientation, a first among universities. He has continued his work into his late 80s.

Dr. Christy Duan is a resident doctor training in psychiatry at Northwell Health in Great Neck, New York. She was an early supporter and an editor on this project.

Michigan State University journalism professor **Richard Epps** worked with graphics students who produced the charts in this guide.

The Bias Busters series is sustained by the consistent and enthusiastic support of Journalism School director and professor **Lucinda Davenport**.

Foreword

By Susan Horowitz

Words always matter. At their core, who has the power to define and convey them has often been the cause of war and peace throughout recorded history.

Over the course of the past 50 years, LGBTQ+ people have overcome the isolation of the closet, undertaken the building of community, often against all odds, and taken the opportunity to be at the table in the halls of government and business, challenging stereotypes and stigma along the way.

LGBTQ+ people first shouted "Gay is good" when they marched in Philadelphia and Washington, D.C., in the late 1960s thanks to pioneers like the late Frank Kameny. Publicly exclaiming this definition of gay went directly to the heart of the bigotry and shaming that had been defining and oppressing gays and lesbians up until this moment. Seeking to be treated like any other citizens, this small band of brave protestors cracked open the closet door, and the world changed forever when it came to defining gay people.

This guide is an extraordinary example of just how far the language has expanded and changed around discussing LGBTQ+ people. In all likelihood, this evolution in our language will continue as people honestly explore the many complex and layered issues that intersect when discussing sexual orientation.

In a time when our country is challenged with cries of "fake news" and what is fact or fiction, we need to be ever more vigilant about who defines us and how they do it.

While LGBTQ+ people no longer allow the heteronormative world to define us, we are a long way from full acceptance. In fact, now more than ever, challenging the language that seeks to do damage is essential.

Galvanizing conversations that allow for a compassionate exploration of the many issues raised in this guide alone will lead to a deeper, more evolved understanding of our fellow human beings.

As the world moves forward, hopefully the opportunity to learn and grow in understanding about these issues will expand and continue to enlighten us. While much progress has been made, we should never become complacent or complicit — especially unwittingly — or we could surely lose the progress we have achieved in recent decades.

Preface

By Dr. David P. Gushee

I am glad to support this important new effort on the part of the Michigan State University School of Journalism to address important basic questions about sexual orientation. As the LGBTQ conversation has evolved with ever-greater complexity, sometimes it can seem like a daunting environment to even begin to enter. Well-intentioned people can fear offending through basic misunderstandings or using terminology in ways that might have been acceptable a while back but not today. So, I am glad for this book, and glad you are reading it.

All human beings share a responsibility to promote fair treatment for everyone. This is one of the most basic moral obligations that there is, and it is articulated in a great many religions and moral belief systems.

It is also widely agreed that basic fairness requires greater effort when it comes to relatively powerless and vulnerable minorities. It is a paradox that is also true — the more a group has been mistreated or marginalized, the more effort is required to ensure that its members receive basic fairness. And there is no question that LGB+ people have been among the most mistreated and marginalized people in many societies.

As a Christian ethicist, I have studied people in many settings who have acted bravely and compassionately on behalf of hated and mistreated groups. My first book was on Christians who rescued Jews during the Holocaust, and since that time I have continually returned to the theme — not because I am so brave, but because I want to be that kind of person in this hard and heartless world.

Essentially, standing up for others, including LGB+ people, involves four steps — seeing, caring, choosing and acting. We must see the suffering of specific others, care about it from the heart, choose to get off the sidelines, and then go ahead and act in ways that the affected group finds most helpful and meaningful. We can be derailed at any point — not noticing (it's amazing how often we don't notice the mistreatment of others that we don't know personally), or noticing and not caring deeply enough, or caring deeply but not choosing to actually do something, or deciding to act but somehow never getting around to it. There is a bit of a gap between each of these steps, which is one reason why it always turns out to be a minority of people who will do anything to stand in solidarity with those who suffer.

Another thing I have learned along the way is that small steps can lead to big steps. Most readers of this book will never become full-blown pro-LGB+ activists out marching in the streets. But anyone can learn more, prepare for those hard conversations with family, friends and co-workers, and be willing to call out egregious examples of hurtful and harmful talk and action when we see it.

It's about a new kind of commitment that goes something like this: I will not stand idly by another day when the well-being of LGB+ people is concerned. I am not looking for a fight, but I also know what I stand for — a world in which people who have been and sometimes still are grossly mistreated can live in peace and wholeness just like others. I will stand up for that kind of world, even when it is uncomfortable.

It's interesting — such a commitment turns out to be hard to segment or limit. As Martin Luther King Jr. liked to say, "A threat to justice anywhere is a threat to justice everywhere." You might find that a deepened commitment to stand up for justice and fairness for LGB+ people will lead you to new horizons in the future. That would be great, because that is what moral growth looks like!

We are living in a transition moment in which socially (often religiously) structured contempt for LGB+ people is being challenged fiercely, first of all by LGB+ people themselves. It is already the case in large sections of American society that anti-LGB+ words and actions are being completely delegitimized, no matter what reasons someone might cite. The trajectory is going in the right direction.

But this is no reason for complacency. It is precisely when prejudice and discrimination against specific groups are in the process of being socially rejected that a shrinking, but increasingly angry, group pushes back hard. Old habits die hard. Old subcultures die harder. We need to drive a stake through the heart of this old, hurtful habit as quickly as we can, because a lot of vulnerable people are still deeply affected by it. All of us have a part to play.

Introduction

This guide is a companion to "100 Questions and Answers About Gender Identity." The need for separate guides illustrates that sexual orientation and gender identity are not the same, and that there are many questions about each dimension.

The creation of this guide at Michigan State University echoes history. On March 7, 1972, East Lansing became the first community in the nation to enact civil rights protections for gay and lesbian people. The effort began with a small group of Michigan State students who called themselves the Gay Liberation Movement. In the fall of 1971, they asked the East Lansing City Council for an ordinance banning discrimination in hiring. The following March it passed, 3-2.

That first ordinance was followed by protections against discrimination in housing, public accommodations and services. Then came prohibitions against discrimination based on gender identity.

But ordinances do not mean acceptance. Lawmakers at state and federal levels have tried to turn back or supersede LGBTQ+ rights adopted across the country. This continues despite recognition of more types of sexuality and increased acceptance by the American public.

It took more than 40 years of work for same-sex marriage to be recognized nationally. It came on June 26, 2015, in a 5-4 ruling by the U.S. Supreme Court. In the majority opinion, Justice Anthony Kennedy wrote, "No union is more profound than marriage, for it embodies the highest ideals of love, fidelity, devotion, sacrifice and family. In forming a marital union, two people become something greater than once they were. As some of the petitioners in these cases demonstrate, marriage embodies a love that may endure even past death. It would misunderstand these men and women to say they disrespect the idea of marriage. Their plea is that they do respect it, respect it so deeply that they seek to find its fulfillment for themselves. ... They ask for equal dignity in the eyes of the law. The Constitution grants them that right."

Michigan State had a footnote to the marriage milestone, as well. The Ingham County clerk, whose courthouse is about 10 miles south of the Michigan State campus, opened up early on a Saturday, the morning after the 2015 decision, to perform one of the nation's first marriages under that ruling. That clerk was Barb Byrum, a former state representative and Michigan State University graduate.

Like the students who petitioned the East Lansing City Council in 1971, the student authors of this guide took the initiative. They formed an independent study team to create it. Guides generally are created by classes of 12-18 students, but these three students showed us again that a small group of people united by a sense of purpose can achieve big things.

Joe Grimm
Series editor
School of Journalism
Michigan State University

Glossary

ally In this context, someone who is not lesbian, gay, bisexual or transgender and who actively supports people who are. The term is also used for people within the LGBTQ+ community who support other LGBTQ+ communities to which they themselves do not belong. The term is useful for groups, activities or campaigns that accept supporters.

asexual Having no sexual attraction or no apparent sex or sex organs. Asexuality is a sexual orientation, not a choice like celibacy, according to the Asexual Visibility & Education Network. It says, "Asexual people have the same emotional needs as everybody else and are just as capable of forming intimate relationships."

biphobia Prejudice, dislike or fear of bisexual people. It questions the legitimacy of bisexuality. Biphobia can occur within the LGBTQ+ community. Biphobic is the adjective form.

bisexual As a noun or adjective, it describes people attracted to more than one gender. Using the noun for individuals can reduce people to just one dimension of their identity. The adjective form, as in "bisexual people," is descriptive but not as limiting.

cisgender A person whose gender identity aligns with the gender they were assigned at birth. In common usage, cisgender usually describes the opposite of being transgender. It does not refer to sexual orientation.

demisexual Needing to have a strong emotional connection with someone before feeling sexual attraction. It does not imply anything about the genders of the people involved.

gay Usually, the adjective for men attracted to men. For women, the term is generally lesbian, though gay is sometimes used as an umbrella term for people with a same-sex orientation. Avoid using gay as a singular noun to refer to someone.

heterosexual Women who are attracted to men and men who are attracted to women. Some prefer the term "straight."

homophobia Fear, hatred or dislike of gay men or lesbians. Homophobic is the adjective. The related label is homophobe, though it can help to use terms that are more precise such as "gay-rights opponent."

homosexual Gay or lesbian is preferred. "Homosexuality" took on a definition associated with the American Psychiatric Association's classification of same-sex attractions as a mental disorder. The group removed the designation in 1973 and this term has largely been replaced by gay and lesbian.

lesbian A woman who is attracted to women. Can be used as a noun or an adjective. Some prefer to be called gay, so it is good to ask.

LGBTQ+ More sexual orientations and gender identities are being recognized all the time. These letters stand for lesbian, gay, bisexual, transgender and queer or questioning. The plus sign means "and more." Some people object to labels in general and this one in particular because it does not cover all sexual orientations. Shared interests and issues bring people and their allies together under this term, which includes gender as well as sexual orientation.

monosexism The assumption that people are attracted to just one gender, or that this way is the norm. This can lead to diminishment or erasure of bisexual people.

pansexual A person who is attracted to all kinds of people, regardless of gender, sex, expression or presentation.

polyamory Romantic or sexual involvement with one or more people, together or separately, with all partners' consent. Similar to ethical non-monogamy.

pride Often used to describe events such as parades that affirm gay identities. Many pride celebrations occur around the June 28 anniversary of a 1969 police raid on the LGBTQ+ friendly Stonewall Inn in New York City that led to riots.

queer People use this term in different ways. Queer can be an umbrella term that includes sexual orientation and gender identity/expression. Some who identify as queer may be gender nonconforming — people who view their identity as beyond the binary of male or female. This word is more acceptable as an adjective than as a noun.

questioning To be unsure of or still figuring out one's sexual orientation.

relationship anarchist One who believes that sexual, romantic, platonic and other relationships with different individuals can have equal prominence. This requires independence, freedom and negotiation. The term was coined in 2012.

romantic orientation Also called affectional or attractional orientation, this is different than sexual orientation but still based on gender. A homoromantic person is attracted to the same sex or gender. A biromantic or panromantic person is romantically attracted to more than one sex or gender. Asexual people can feel romantic attraction. Other kinds of attraction are aesthetic (to appreciate appearance) or sensual (desire for tactile, nonsexual contact such as hugging).

sexual orientation Physical, romantic, emotional or sexual attraction. This can be to members of the same sex or gender, a different one, or more than one.

sexual preference The expression is outdated and can offend. It implies that people chose which sex or gender to be attracted to. This can imply that they need corrective treatment. Actually, attraction has been found to not be a choice. Use sexual orientation instead.

skoliosexual Attraction to transgender or nonbinary people.

transgender This adjective describes someone whose gender identity does not match the one assigned at birth. One can identify as lesbian, gay, bisexual, asexual and a variety of other sexualities in addition to being transgender. Avoid using this term as a noun by referring to someone as "a transgender." This can dehumanize people by making them seem foreign or one-dimensional. Transgender is sometimes shortened to trans.

transition This can mean external actions. They include hormone treatments, surgical procedures, or a change in one's name and pronouns such as she and hers or he and his. Most transgender people do not undergo surgery. Transitioning begins with the internal process of discovering and accepting one's gender identity.

transphobia Dislike or aversion to people who are transgender.

transsexual A term considered by some to be offensive and outdated, it refers to people who use or consider using medical interventions to physically change the expression of their gender.

For more on these issues, see our companion guide, "100 Questions and Answers About Gender Identity," or the resources at the end of this guide.

More on Terms

1 How many sexual orientations are there?

Sexual orientations include but are not limited to asexual, pansexual, lesbian, bisexual, gay, heterosexual, demisexual, homosexual and skoliosexual. The English language is fluid, with new identifiers arising and previous ones changing all the time. This area is one of rapid change right now.

2 Does everyone fit into a category?

Not everyone finds a specific category that suits them, so new terms are being introduced. Some people are moving away from identifiers or labels altogether. Labels can seem to set categories for life, which is not always the reality. People who are discovering their sexuality or identity sometimes describe themselves as "questioning."

3 Are bisexual and pansexual the same?

While the terms have different meanings, there is some overlap in usage. Bisexuality means to be attracted to males and females. Some people who fit this description call themselves pansexual. It describes people with various levels of attraction for people of all gender identities or expressions.

4 What does heteronormativity mean?

Heteronormativity is when people, institutions and social structures set opposite-sex orientation as the norm. Media including television, movies and books that focus solely on heterosexual main characters and relationships perpetuate this. People reinforce heteronormativity in everyday ways such as in their language or assumptions about the gender of someone's partner. The assumptions are often made with no ill will. It takes awareness and effort to overcome assumptions.

5 What about homonormativity?

Homonormativity is a perceived norm among LGBTQ+ people. It is a hierarchy of identities. White, middle-class, cisgender gay men are often depicted as the standard. Statistically, they generally have more resources. This creates a limited picture of people in the group and can delegitimize or obscure other identities. For example, lower socioeconomic, transgender lesbians of color are often left out of the picture.

6 Why do some people say "queer" or "faggot" with pride?

These words have been used to ridicule and ostracize people, even when their sexuality is not known. These terms and others like them carry negative connotations. Using "gay" as an insult, or to put something down as being "so gay" is to use that word as a pejorative. Some people have been reclaiming words to empower themselves. The Human Rights Campaign announced in 2016 it would add Q to LGBT, recognizing the word when used as a positive. Especially when used by people who are not LGBTQ+, the words still can offend.

7 What is intersectionality?

When people have more than one social identity that is subject to discrimination or oppression, those identities create a new one distinct from any of its components. Intersectionality includes combinations of identities such as sexual orientation, ability, gender, class, ethnicity, race, religion and age. An example would be a Black lesbian. Civil rights activist Kimberlé Crenshaw coined the term for people who have more than one marginalized identity.

8 What does it mean to be privileged?

This means having automatic advantages because of one's characteristics. Privilege can come from one's socioeconomic status, religion, ability, gender, race or sexual orientation. Having privilege does not mean that a person either did or did not work to get where they are; it means they have more opportunities. Because one's family and close social circles might share the same privileges, it can be hard to recognize them as out of the ordinary.

Identity

9 What percentage of Americans are lesbian, gay or bi?

An estimated 10 million people in the United States identify as LGBTQ+, according to a 2016 survey by the Gallup polling organization. That's just a little more than 4 percent of the population. But reluctance to identify oneself in these ways may result in an undercount. Researchers at the UCLA School of Law's Williams Institute have found that people in the United States are more likely to say they have experienced same-sex attraction or activity than to use a label. Many factors can affect the ways and willingness of people to disclose their sexual orientations. Those include how safe and comfortable they feel doing so. The U.S. Census Bureau told Congress the 2020 count would begin asking couples if they were "same-sex" or "opposite-sex." The bureau soon retracted that plan.

10 What is known about numbers for different sexualities?

According to the Williams Institute, just more than 1 percent of U.S. men identify as gay, and almost

1.5 percent identify as bisexual. Just more than 1 percent of women identify as lesbian; about twice as many identify as bisexual. Research on asexuality is limited, though some researchers have estimated that 1 percent of the world's population identifies as asexual.

11 How is the LGBTQ+ population distributed by race?

According to a 2017 survey by Gallup, 3.6 percent of White people in the United States and 4.6 percent of Blacks identified as LGBTQ+. Five percent of Asian Americans and 5.4 percent of Hispanic Americans did.

12 Are gay men more feminine and lesbians more masculine?

This question is about stereotypes. The answer depends not just on how people present themselves, but on how others expect them to express their gender. A person's degree of masculinity or femininity is called gender expression. Society assigns masculine and feminine behaviors. Men judged to behave in feminine ways might be assumed to be gay. The same can be said for women whose expression is more masculine. However, according to the Trevor Project, everyone has both masculine and feminine qualities. The Trevor Project describes spectrums for sexual orientation, gender and expression or behavior. Individuals can be anywhere along these spectrums. Some propose that the range is not simply linear from one place to another.

The LGBT population

Percentage of Pew Research sample of LGBT adults who describe themselves as...

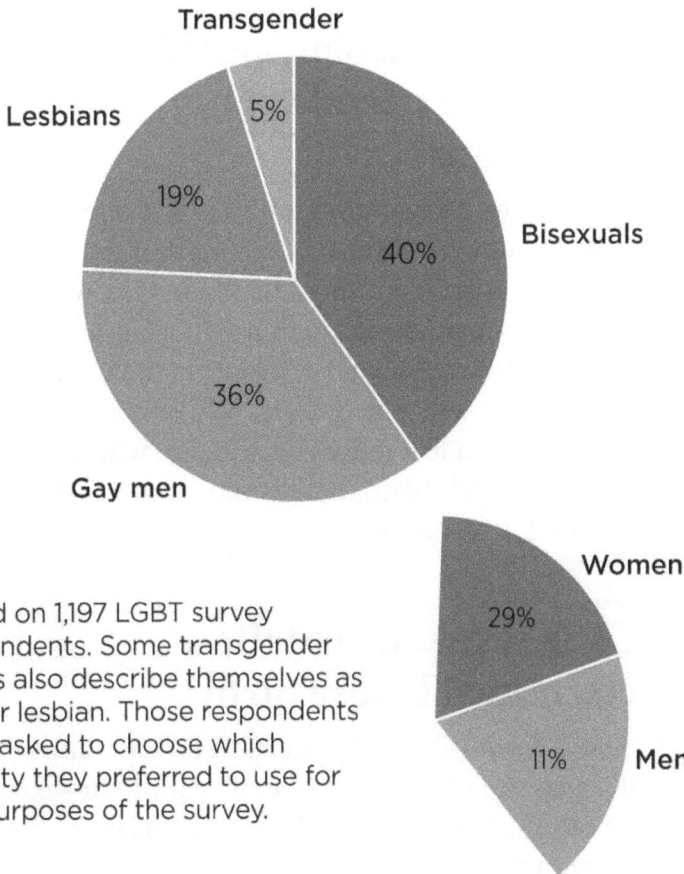

Transgender

Lesbians

Bisexuals

5%

19%

40%

36%

Gay men

Women

29%

11% **Men**

Based on 1,197 LGBT survey respondents. Some transgender adults also describe themselves as gay or lesbian. Those respondents were asked to choose which identity they preferred to use for the purposes of the survey.

Source: Pew Research Center, 2013

Graphic by Claire Barkholz

13 Do bisexual people tend to present more masculine or feminine than people of other orientations?

This confuses sexual orientation and gender identity or expression. Like people of any sexual orientation, bisexual people can present as masculine, feminine or androgynous and to varying degrees.

14 Do gay, lesbian and bisexual people have friends of only those orientations?

Of course not. Sexual orientation is just one dimension of who we are. People have friends who are different from them in all kinds of ways. Naturally, they might share more interests with people of the same sexual orientation than with people of different orientations. While it is natural for all people to feel more comfortable with people who understand them, there is more to us than just our sexual orientation.

15 Is sexual orientation determined before birth?

Researchers at Johns Hopkins University found little evidence of a biological explanation for sexual orientation. More research is needed to clarify environmental factors.

16 Can sexual orientation change?

A University of Utah researcher reports that, for some people, sexual orientation does change. According to research by Dr. Lisa Diamond, 10 to 14 percent of women and 6 to 9 percent of men experience changes in sexual orientation.

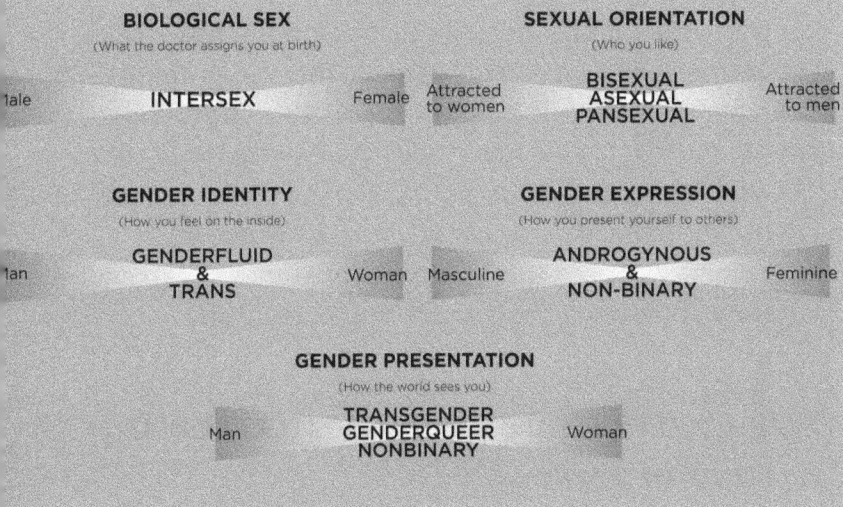

Art by: Terri Powys   Source: The Trevor Project

The Spectrum:

BIOLOGICAL SEX
(What the doctor assigns you at birth)

Male   INTERSEX   Female

SEXUAL ORIENTATION
(Who you like)

Attracted to women   BISEXUAL / ASEXUAL / PANSEXUAL   Attracted to men

GENDER IDENTITY
(How you feel on the inside)

Man   GENDERFLUID & TRANS   Woman

GENDER EXPRESSION
(How you present yourself to others)

Masculine   ANDROGYNOUS & NON-BINARY   Feminine

GENDER PRESENTATION
(How the world sees you)

Man   TRANSGENDER / GENDERQUEER / NONBINARY   Woman

Visibility

17 Are lesbian, gay and bisexual people socially accepted in the United States?

Acceptance is growing. In 2016 the nonpartisan Pew Research Center reported that 63 percent of U.S. adults said society should accept homosexuality. Twenty-eight percent disagreed. This varies among religious and political groups. On the issue of same-sex marriage, Pew reported that 62 percent of U.S. adults were accepting and 32 percent were opposed in 2017. That was a reversal from 2001 when 57 percent opposed same-sex marriage and 35 percent were accepting. The balance tipped in 2011.

18 Are some races more accepting than others?

A 2013 Pew study found that White LGBT Americans were more likely than non-White LGBT people to say society is becoming more accepting. One area of tension had to do with religion. LGBT people of color reported experiencing more conflict between their sexual orientation and religion than White LGBT people.

Feelings on same-sex marriage by generation

The increase in the share of adults who favor same-sex marriage is due in part to generational change. Younger generations express higher levels of support for same-sex marriage.

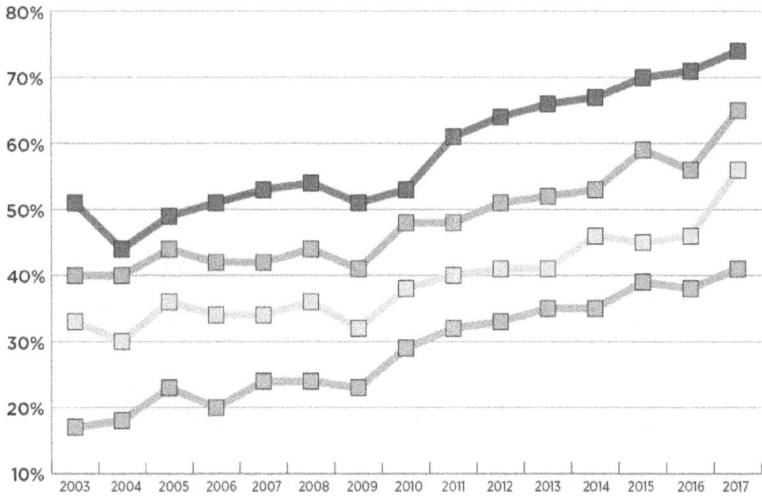

- ■ Millennials (1981 or later)
- ▣ Generation X (1965-80)
- ☐ Baby Boomers (1946-64)
- ▥ Silent Generation (1928-45)

Source: Pew research   Graphic by Riley Murdock

19 How does the United States compare on acceptance?

These were the 11 most accepting countries of lesbians and gays, according to a 2014 Gallup survey of 124 countries.

Netherlands	87 percent
Spain	87 percent
Canada	84 percent
Belgium	82 percent
Norway	80 percent
Luxemburg	79 percent
Uruguay	79 percent
Sweden	78 percent
Ireland	77 percent
United Kingdom	77 percent
Denmark	76 percent

The United States was at 53 percent in 2014. It was at 60 percent early in 2016 in a similar Gallup poll.

20 Is acceptance growing?

In some places, yes. A Pew survey in 2013 found majority acceptance in North America, the European Union and much of Latin America. However, there was a strong correlation between religion and rejection in some countries. The survey found rejection rates of 90 percent or more in some Muslim and African nations.

21 Who are some important lesbian, gay and bisexual public figures?

Media

Anderson Cooper Primary CNN news anchor of "Anderson Cooper 360," he was an established journalist before publicly coming out in 2012. He became the first openly gay moderator of a presidential debate in 2016.

Ellen DeGeneres Comedian, talk show host and the voice of Disney Pixar character Dory in "Finding Nemo" and "Finding Dory." DeGeneres publicly came out on her sitcom "Ellen" in 1997. This made her the first gay lead character on American network television. She has remained a prominent LGBTQ+ rights spokesperson and activist.

Don Lemon A CNN anchor, he disclosed his sexual orientation in his memoir, "Transparent." Lemon told The New York Times that his journalistic obligation to be honest led him to bring his sexual orientation to light.

Rachel Maddow Host of MSNBC's Emmy Award-winning "The Rachel Maddow Show," she has been a political commentator, radio host and author. Maddow came out as lesbian at age 17 in the college newspaper at Stanford University.

Robin Roberts An anchor on "Good Morning America," Roberts wrote a post in 2013 about her battle with cancer and a blood disorder. In it, she acknowledged her longtime girlfriend.

Ruby Rose Australian model, DJ and television personality Rose gained fame with her role on the Netflix Original Series "Orange is the New Black." Rose identifies as gender-fluid and came out as lesbian at age 12. Her androgyny pushed boundaries and increased visibility.

Entertainment

Margaret Cho Comedian, actress, author, fashion designer and singer-songwriter, she came to prominence with the ABC sitcom "All-American Girl." She created and starred in the show. Cho is best known for her stand-up routines.

Chris Colfer Actor and writer best known for his role as Kurt Hummel on the TV show "Glee" (2009-2015), Colfer became a role model for adolescents. His character was partially based on his experience as a young, openly gay man.

Jodie Foster Actress, director and producer Foster received an Oscar nomination at age 12 for her portrayal of a child prostitute in Martin Scorsese's 1976 film "Taxi Driver." She won a Golden Globe and Academy Award for "The Accused" and starred in "The Silence of the Lambs."

Neil Patrick Harris Actor and comedian Harris came out in response to media rumors in 2006. Following the passage of New York's Marriage Equality Act, Harris and David Burtka married.

Rosie O'Donnell Actress, comedian and television personality O'Donnell came out two months after playing a lesbian character on the sitcom "Will and Grace." She did it during a 2002 benefit. O'Donnell said she wanted her coming out to play a role in advocating for adoptions by same-sex couples.

Wanda Sykes She has been a comedian, a writer on "The Chris Rock Show," an actor on TV and in films and a voice character. Entertainment Weekly recognized Sykes as one of the 25 funniest people in America in 2004.

George Takei Author, Broadway and television actor, he played "Mr. Sulu," helmsman of the USS Enterprise in the TV series "Star Trek." Takei is an activist with a social media following of millions.

Lily Tomlin She has acted for television, movies, cable video and Broadway. Credits include the comedy TV series "Laugh-In" (1969-1973) and the movies "Nashville" and "Nine to Five." She won a Tony for her one-woman Broadway show, "The Search for Signs of Intelligent Life in the Universe."

Music

Lance Bass In addition to singing in the '90s pop band NSYNC, Bass is a dancer, actor and film and music producer. In 2006, he came out to People Magazine. That year he received the Human Rights Campaign's Visibility Award.

Brandi Carlile She taught herself to play the piano and guitar, inspired by Elton John classics. She is a writer, musician and singer in folk, rock and country genres. Her single, "The Story," has been used on numerous TV shows.

Beth Ditto This singer-songwriter's voice has been compared to those of Etta James, Janis Joplin and Tina Turner. She worked with the indie rock group Gossip.

Melissa Ferrick Proficient at vocals, guitar, bass guitar, percussion and flugelhorn, she addresses LGB issues in her music. The Gay and Lesbian American Music Association named her album "Everything I Need" Album of the Year in 1999.

Tyler Glenn Lead singer for American pop band Neon Trees, Glenn came out to Rolling Stone magazine in 2014. Glenn was raised in The Church of Jesus Christ of Latter-Day Saints but disassociated. In 2016, his solo album explored his sexuality and relationship with religion.

Indigo Girls Amy Ray and **Emily Saliers** met in elementary school in Georgia and began playing together in high school. They have recorded scores of songs under major labels and their own and they have toured. They have been recognized for championing gay rights, the environment and the rights of Native Americans.

Elton John An award-winning singer and songwriter, John came out as bisexual in 1976. Following his divorce in 1988, he came out as gay. John has used his fame to create visibility for the LGBTQ+ community. During the AIDS epidemic in the 1980s, he advocated for people living with HIV. In 25 years, the Elton John AIDS Foundation raised more than $200 million for HIV research.

Adam Lambert Known for his theatrical performances, Lambert finished as runner-up in season eight of "American Idol" in 2009. In 2012, he became the first openly gay artist to top the charts with his album "Trespassing."

Ricky Martin Latin American singer Martin brought

Latin pop music into the U.S. music scene in his 1999 Grammy performance. He then released "Livin' la Vida Loca." That opened a door for Spanish-speaking artists to transition into the English-speaking music market. After coming out in 2010, Martin founded the nonprofit Ricky Martin Foundation to advocate for children around the world.

Frank Ocean Singer, songwriter and rapper Ocean came out in a letter posted on Tumblr in 2012. This became a pivotal moment for hip-hop music. It encouraged a new generation of musicians and young people to tell their stories.

Raven-Symone An actress, singer, songwriter, rapper, dancer, panelist and producer, she got her start on NBC's "The Cosby Show." Film credits include "Dr. Dolittle," "Dr. Dolittle 2" and "College Road Trip." She has appeared on "Empire," "Black-ish" and ABC's talk show "The View."

Sports

Jason Collins He played in the National Basketball Association for 13 seasons before retiring in 2014. In 2013, Collins came out in a cover story for Sports Illustrated. He was the first athlete from one of the four major North American team sports leagues to do so. Collins said he chose jersey number 98 in memory of the 1998 murder of Matthew Shepard, a gay student.

Brittney Griner She plays for the Phoenix Mercury in the Women's National Basketball Association. She was a three-time All-America player for Baylor and the first NCAA basketball player to score 2,000 points and block 500 shots. Griner was also the first openly gay athlete to have an endorsement contract with Nike.

Greg Louganis The U.S. Olympic diver who won double gold medals at the 1984 and 1988 games, he came out in a taped announcement shown at the opening ceremony of the 1994 Gay Games. In 1995, he announced he was HIV-positive. He became a human rights advocate and continued to mentor swimmers.

Martina Navratilova Tennis magazine named her the world's best female tennis player from 1975 to 2005. She won more Grand Slam titles than any other player, male or female. She publicly identified as bisexual in 1981 and later as lesbian.

Diana Nyad The long-distance swimmer circled Manhattan, swam from the Bahamas to Florida and, at age 64, became the first to swim 110 miles from Cuba to Florida without a shark cage. She has become an author, journalist and motivational speaker

Megan Rapinoe and **Abby Wambach** They won gold with the 2012 U.S. Women's Olympics team. In the 2011 World Cup quarter finals, Rapinoe sent a 45-year crossing pass to Wambach, whose header has been called one of the greatest goals in women's soccer.

Adam Rippon and **Gus Kenworthy** They became the first openly gay U.S. Olympians in 2018. Other athletes had competed in previous Olympics Games, but came out afterward.

Michael Sam When Sam was drafted by the St. Louis Rams in 2014, he become the first openly gay player to be drafted by the National Football League. He played for the Dallas Cowboys. When he briefly joined the Montreal Alouettes in 2015, he became the first openly gay player in the Canadian Football League. He retired that year for mental health reasons.

Katie Sowers An assistant coach for the San Francisco 49ers, she came out as lesbian in 2017, making her the first openly LGBTQ+ coach in U.S. men's professional sports.

Johnny Weir Three-time U.S. champion, two-time Olympian and World Championships bronze medalist figure skater, Weir came out in his 2011 biography, "Welcome to My World." Weir was selected as grand marshal of the 2011 Los Angeles Pride Parade and has become a pop-culture superstar.

22 What does the rainbow flag symbolize?

Called the gay pride flag, it represents pride and diversity. It is a rainbow of horizontal stripes with red on top, followed by orange, yellow, green, blue and purple. The original gay pride flag was created in 1978 by San Francisco artist Gilbert Baker and a team including tie-dye artist Lynn Segerblom and James McNamara, who sewed it. That flag also had pink and turquoise stripes. Other identities also have flags.

23 What is the difference between tolerance and acceptance?

This is a matter of degree and is part of the rights discussion. At a 2015 Human Rights Campaign gala, "Orange is the New Black" actress Samira Wiley laid it out: "How little we must think of ourselves, to only accept tolerance. What about acceptance? What about celebration, and love, and embracing difference, rather than merely tolerating it? What might happen if we raise the bar higher?"

24 Are LGBTQ+ people depicted on TV, cable and streaming video?

GLAAD monitors TV portrayals annually. Its 2017 "Where We Are on TV" report made several observations. The percentage of regularly scheduled gay, lesbian, bisexual, transgender and/or queer characters was at an all-time high of 6.4 percent. Broadcast, cable and streaming originals lacked LGBTQ+ characters of color. Seventy-seven percent of the 70 characters were White. For the first time, GLAAD was able to count asexual characters.

Coming Out

25 What does the expression "come out" mean?

This means to accept one's own marginalized sexual orientation and to then tell others. Coming out usually occurs in stages. People often come out to friends first, then family, then coworkers or peers. The order depends on whom the person is most comfortable telling. The process never really ends because people must decide whether to come out when they make new friends or change jobs or schools. Increasing visibility of others who share one's identity can make coming out easier.

26 What does it mean to be "in the closet?"

Someone who is closeted has not yet disclosed their sexual orientation. It is possible to be out with some people but closeted with others. Some people who have a bad experience coming out might go back to being closeted.

27 Why do people decide they will come out?

Coming out is a very personal decision. San Francisco State University's Family Acceptance Project says that the timing and method should be up to the individual. Sometimes people feel secure enough in their identity to come out to their family and friends. Some people choose to come out in their work life and not their personal life, or vice versa. People can be discouraged by social stigma, fear of discrimination, physical harm, violation or death, limits on opportunities and a lack of role models.

28 On average, at what age do people come out?

The average age is 14 to 16, according to the Family Acceptance Project. This is younger than in the 1970s, when the average age was the early to mid-20s.

29 What are the steps in coming out?

Steps include planning what to say, forming a support group and deciding whom to tell first. One must also be ready for negative reactions.

The coming out experience:
When you thought, knew, told

Median ages at which gay men/lesbians/bisexuals say they first thought, knew for sure or told someone they were or might be LGB.

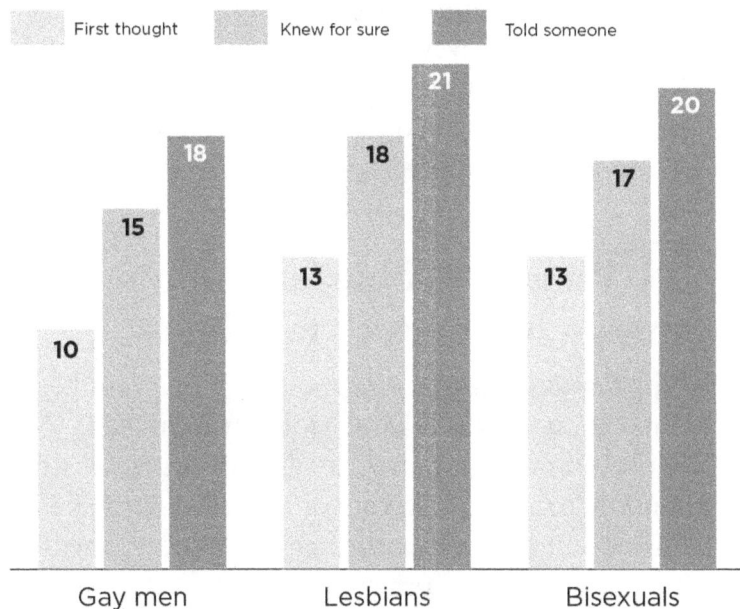

First thought   Knew for sure   Told someone

Gay men: 10, 15, 18
Lesbians: 13, 18, 21
Bisexuals: 13, 17, 20

Based on 398 gay men, 277 lesbians and 479 bisexuals. Median ages are computed based on those who answered each question. Those who are still not sure they are LGB, those who have not yet told someone and those who did not answer the questions are removed from the analysis of the relevant questions.

Source: Pew Research Center, 2013   Graphic by Geneva Swanson

30 At what age do people know their sexual orientation?

People come to terms with their sexual orientation at varying stages. While it is common for people to know their sexual orientation at a young age, they may not actually come out then. Coming out is encouraged or discouraged by many factors including whether there is support from family and friends or schoolmates. Religion can be a factor. Often, younger people are discouraged from expressing a same-sex orientation because they're "too young." However, young people typically are not challenged for expressing attraction to the opposite sex. Sexual attraction does not mean someone is having sexual relations.

31 What are some fears about coming out to one's family?

Many fear rejection or disappointing their families. Some relatives have reacted violently or kicked people out of their homes. A Williams Institute study found that about 40 percent of homeless teens are LGBTQ+. It is important for people to be met with support when they come out.

32 What does it mean to "out" someone?

Outing is to reveal someone else's orientation before that individual is ready to come out. Outing can occur after the individual has already come out, but not publicly or to everyone. People out others in gossip, out of malice or ignorance. Outing has also been done by other LGBTQ+ people who believe others should come out, too. Sometimes they are looking for support. Outing occasionally has been very public. For instance, some gay politicians who professed to be anti-gay have been outed by people trying to expose hypocrisy.

33 Why is outing someone a problem?

Outing a person denies their right to tell their story themselves in the way they would like. It also deprives them of choosing the timing or person they would like to disclose the information to first.

34 How can you support someone who comes out to you?

Caitlin Taylor, one of the authors of this guide, wrote about this for "Her Campus" at Michigan State University. When someone comes out, recognize their courage and show support. Continue to do the same activities together, and include them in your plans. It is crucial to not pass judgment and to respect their right to share their story themselves.

35 What is National Coming Out Day?

This is celebrated on Oct. 11. It observes the anniversary of the 1987 National March on Washington for Lesbian and Gay Rights. According to the Human Rights Campaign, the day recognizes coming out as a tool for visibility.

Relationships

36 How is dating different in the LGBTQ+ community?

It can be more difficult for LGBTQ+ people to find each other because the number of gay people is smaller and there can be risks in disclosing their orientation. People date in many different ways. This is not determined by sexuality.

37 How do LGBTQ+ people find others to date?

Dating for LGBTQ+ people is similar to dating among straight people, but the pool is smaller. Just as not all straight people meet others in bars, in school or at work, LGBTQ+ people find their dates in different ways, too.

38 Do dating apps help?

Dating apps can be especially helpful when the pool is small and dispersed. Some dating apps are exclusively for LGBTQ+ people. Some apps allow people to search by sexual orientation. Apps such as Tinder, Zoosk, Her and Grindr are popular. According to a Match.com survey, 70 percent of gay men and 47 percent of lesbians have been in a relationship with someone they met online.

39 Does bisexuality give people more choices in dating?

Not necessarily. Being attracted to people of more than one gender does not mean more options. Finding someone with whom one shares an attraction can be difficult, and many people do not want to be in a relationship with someone who is bisexual. In a 2016 survey of 1,000 adults, sex toy retailer Adam and Eve found that 47 percent of respondents said that they would not date a bisexual person.

40 What does it mean to experiment?

Experimenting refers to an individual trying something new sexually. This could be a first partner, a partner of a gender they have not been intimate with or a number of other firsts.

41 Can asexual people be in relationships?

Of course. Like other kinds of sexuality, asexuality is a spectrum. A person can be asexual and still have sexual or romantic relationships.

42 Is it OK to ask LGBTQ+ people about their sex lives?

People have sex in different ways. The answers from one person would be so intimate and individual that they could not then be generalized. As a general rule, people's sex lives are private matters and should be respected as such. The answers are very personal, they are not simple and asking the question can seem to minimize other aspects of relationships.

43 Do gays and lesbians ever date the opposite gender?

Many gays and lesbians have romantic or sexual relationships or marriages with people of another gender. This does not invalidate their identity. Some might date another gender after coming out, too. It is important to remember that sexuality is fluid and nonbinary. Sexual orientation is about attraction, not just behavior. People who have not dated or engaged in sexual activity can still be gay or bisexual.

44 Do same-sex couples designate masculine and feminine roles?

Roles might seem a required part to someone used to binary relationships, but they are not necessary. Some people assume such roles, but not everyone does. Designating feminine and masculine roles mirrors heterosexual relationships, which is unnecessary in same-sex relationships. Some people do not use specific gender roles at all.

Families

45 In parenting, do same-sex couples have a "mom" and a "dad"?

Same-sex couples with children need not have a designated "mom" and "dad," just as they need not designate one "wife" and one "husband." Many same-sex couples refer to themselves as two husbands or two wives. The fact that one partner calls the other his husband does not mean that he is not also a husband. So, some families have two moms or two dads. It's best to ask or listen for conversational cues.

46 Can same-sex couples have children of their own?

Yes. Males can have a child using one partner's sperm and an egg donor/surrogate to carry the child. Females can have a baby using a sperm donor and fertilization methods such as in-vitro or intrauterine insemination to implant the fertilized egg in one partner's uterus. They can also use a surrogate.

47 How many children have same-sex parents?

The American Association for Marriage and Family Therapy estimates 1 million to 9 million children have at least one parent who is gay or lesbian. The 2011 American Community Survey found that 15 percent of same-sex couples have children in their households. It is difficult to get an accurate count because many people decline to disclose their sexual orientation for surveys.

48 How many same-sex couples adopt?

An estimated 16,000 same-sex couples were raising more than 22,000 adopted children in the United States according to a 2013 report by the Williams Institute. Same-sex couples are four times more likely than other couples to have adopted children. Ten percent of children with same-sex parents are adopted.

49 Is it difficult for same-sex couples to adopt?

This is in flux. It had been getting easier, but federal and state legislation in 2018 was designed to discourage such adoptions. Some states have restricted adoption, foster care, custody and visitation rights based on sexual orientation. Adoption by same-sex couples was not legal in all 50 states until 2016. Stereotypes and ideas about morality and safety support the belief that heterosexual couples are better parents than same-sex ones. Research has disproved that.

50 Is it harmful for children to have same-sex parents?

Seventy-nine studies have found that children of gay or lesbian parents do as well as children in other kinds of families. The findings come from a Columbia Law School review of scholarly research through 2017. It concurred with a 2016 study in the Journal of Developmental and Behavioral Health. This study found that children of same-sex parents are as emotionally and physically healthy as children of different-sex parents. They can be more likely to talk about emotionally difficult topics and are often more resilient, compassionate and tolerant. This is from the American Association for Marriage and Family Therapy.

Health

51 What are top health issues for lesbian, gay and bisexual people?

Lesbian and bisexual women experience some unique barriers to health care. These include lower rates of insurance, fear of discrimination and negative experiences. Also, because female sexual health care focuses on reproduction, there are fewer or later entry points into the health-care system. These contribute to later detection and higher rates of breast, endometrial and ovarian cancers in lesbian and bi women. Other conditions are polycystic ovary syndrome, or PCOS, and depression or anxiety.

For gay and bisexual men, the Centers for Disease Control and Prevention reports that homophobia, stigma and discrimination can harm health. It reports that they experience higher rates than other men of HIV and other sexually transmitted diseases, depression and tobacco and drug use.

52 How long do lesbian and gay people live compared to the general population?

Life expectancies for gay and straight people are about the same, according to the Southern Poverty Law Center. This is despite higher rates of suicide and HIV/AIDS for gay people. Life expectancy for U.S. men is about 76 and for women it is about 81.

53 Why was HIV/AIDS first called a "gay disease?"

When the HIV/AIDS epidemic broke out in the United States in June 1981, people did not understand its cause or seriousness. The disease was briefly and initially called GRID, for gay-related immune deficiency. Because it hit gay men and intravenous drug users first, people stigmatized the disease according to those who caught it and did not pursue its cause. This further stigmatized those who got the disease and slowed down public notice of it. President Ronald Reagan did not publicly address the epidemic or dedicate significant research funds to it until 1987. By then, hundreds of thousands of Americans had become infected or died. The disease changed the national dialogue about sex, sexuality and, later, issues of socioeconomic status and access to health care.

54 How much of the population with HIV/AIDS is gay?

This is difficult to say because of whether and how people report their sexuality in surveys. However, there are good data on those who are diagnosed. About 70 percent of new HIV infections diagnosed every year are among gay and bisexual men. More than 600,000 of these men are living with HIV. The Centers for Disease Control and Prevention reported in 2018 that Black and African-American men who had sex with other men accounted for 26 percent of the 39,782 new HIV diagnoses in the United States in 2016. This is the most-at-risk population for HIV.

55 Is HIV/AIDS declining?

From 2004 to 2015, HIV diagnoses in the United States declined 19 percent overall but increased 6 percent among gay and bisexual men, according to the Centers for Disease Control and Prevention. The increases were primarily among African-American and Hispanic/Latino men. Education and prevention efforts are being used to combat the crisis and eliminate stigma.

56 What are the restrictions on people donating blood?

The Red Cross follows Federal Drug Administration guidelines. These say men who have had sex with another man should not give blood for 12 months, even if they are monogamous. Critics say deferrals are not necessary. They say advances in HIV testing have reduced the risk of transmitting the virus through transfusions. There are no deferrals for women or for transgender people and there are no longer lifetime bans.

57 Is being gay a mental illness?

Homosexuality was characterized as a mental disorder by the American Psychiatric Association's first Diagnostic and Statistical Manual of Mental Disorders, DSM-1, in 1952. The designation was removed in 1973's DSM-III after a review of scientific evidence presented by gay and lesbian activists. The change was agreed to by several committees, the association's trustees and its membership.

58 Are there other mental health concerns?

Gay and bisexual men are more likely to experience depression, generalized anxiety disorder and bipolar disorder, according to the Centers for Disease Control and Prevention. This is attributed to homophobia, stigma and discrimination. Lesbian and bisexual women are more likely to have depression or an anxiety disorder, according to the U.S. Department of Health and Human Services. These concerns are seen as contributing to higher suicide rates among gay people.

59 What is the suicide attempt rate among lesbian, gay and bisexual youth?

According to the 2015 National Youth Risk Behavior Survey, 34.9 percent of gay, lesbian, bisexual or questioning students were planning suicide. Almost 25 percent had attempted it in the previous year. Of straight teens in the study, 11.9 percent said they had been planning suicide, and 6.3 percent said they had tried it in the prior year. A study in the Journal of the American Medical Association found that suicide rates went down in states that allowed same-sex marriage.

60 What is conversion therapy?

Conversion therapy is a discredited practice purporting to alter a person's sexual orientation or gender identity. Medical practitioners and mental health organizations have rejected it. In 2007, the American Psychological Association reviewed extensive research and concluded it showed that conversion therapy does not work and is harmful. By 2017, 15 states, and the District of Columbia had passed laws restricting conversion therapy for minors, according to the Human Rights Campaign.

Safety

61 What share of hate crimes are about sexual orientation?

For 2016, FBI Uniform Crime Statistics reported that 16.7 percent of 6,063 single-bias incidents were over real or perceived sexual orientation. More than half targeted gay males. Crimes included intimidation, assault, aggravated assault and property crimes.

Single-bias incidents

Analysis of the 5,618 single-bias incidents reported in 2015 revealed that:

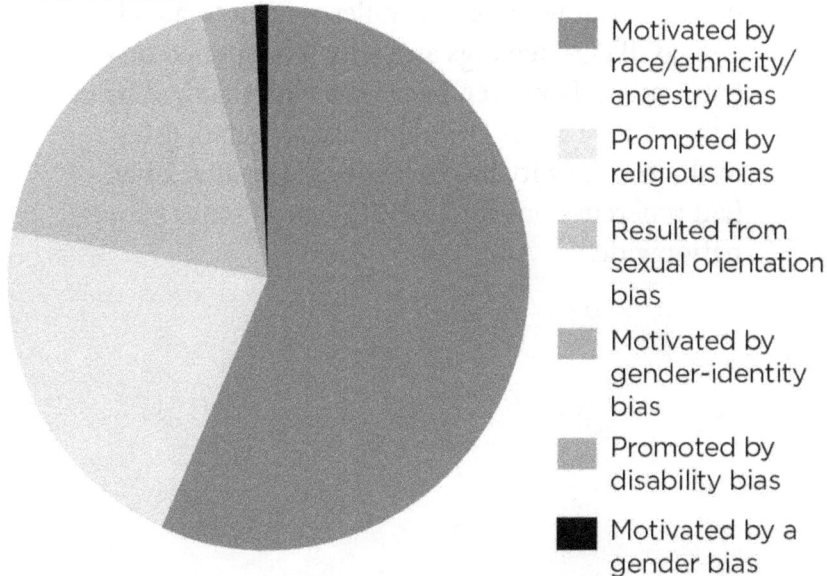

- Motivated by race/ethnicity/ancestry bias
- Prompted by religious bias
- Resulted from sexual orientation bias
- Motivated by gender-identity bias
- Promoted by disability bias
- Motivated by a gender bias

Source: 2015 FBI hate crime statistics

Graphic by John Lavaccare

62 How are gay people treated by law enforcement?

About three-fourths of 2,376 LGBTQ+ people in a 2014 Williams Institute survey reported contact with police in the previous five years. Of those, 21 percent reported hostile behaviors from officers and 14 percent reported verbal assault. About 3 percent reported sexual harassment and 2 percent reported physical assault.

63 What was the significance of the 2016 Orlando massacre?

On June 12, 2016, 49 people were killed and 53 wounded at Pulse, an LGBTQ+ nightclub in Orlando. The massacre was the deadliest U.S. mass shooting until that time by a single shooter. There has been debate about whether the killer was motivated by anti-LGBTQ+ feelings and why it happened on Latin night. However, because a club that had been a haven for LGBTQ+ people was targeted, grief in the community has been deep. The attack has had repercussions for LGBTQ+ and Latino people nationwide.

School and Work

64 What is the school environment like for LGBTQ+ students?

When the Human Rights Campaign published a 2016 report on these students, it was titled "Like Walking Through a Hailstorm." According to the report, content on bullying, harassment and LGBTQ+ topics was missing from school curricula and resources. It also reported that LGBTQ+ student groups were discriminated against. Discrimination and bigotry were reported as coming from classmates and school personnel. It occurred on the basis of both sexuality and gender identity.

65 Are gay students bullied more than others?

According to GLSEN's 2015 National School Climate Survey, 85.2 percent of LGBTQ+ students said they had been verbally bullied. Nearly 35 percent of them reported physical bullying. Almost 49 percent experienced cyberbullying. Students in the survey said anti-bullying education helps, especially when it specifically addresses LGBTQ+ bullying. For comparison, the National Center for Educational Statistics reported in 2016 that 20.8 percent of students in the general population said they had been bullied.

66 Do schools teach about LGBTQ+ people and issues?

The 2015 National School Climate Study asked students about this. Sixty-three percent said classes just did not include these topics. Of those who said it was taught, 22.4 percent said the issues were taught in a positive way and 17.9 percent said they were covered in a negative way. English, history and social studies classes were most often mentioned as including such content. Most students said they did get information about LGBTQ+ topics at school in the library, internet or textbooks and readings. Most students said they could identify at least one supportive staff member.

67 Is sexual health for non-heterosexuals taught in schools?

GLSEN and other organizations have called for greater attention to sexual health education. According to GLSEN, "19 percent of U.S. secondary schools provide curricula or supplementary sex education materials that are LGBTQ-inclusive."

Frequency that LGBTQ students hear anti-gay remarks at school

	Never	Rarely	Sometimes	Often	Frequently
"That's so gay"	1.9%	9.3%	21.3%	27%	40.4%
Remarks about gender expression	4.3%	9.4%	23.4%	29.3%	33.6%
Other homophopic remarks	4.2%	14%	23.1%	24.3%	34.5%
Remarks about transgender people	14.3%	19.2%	25.9%	19.5%	21%
"No Homo"	7.6%	24%	29.6%	21.3%	17.4%

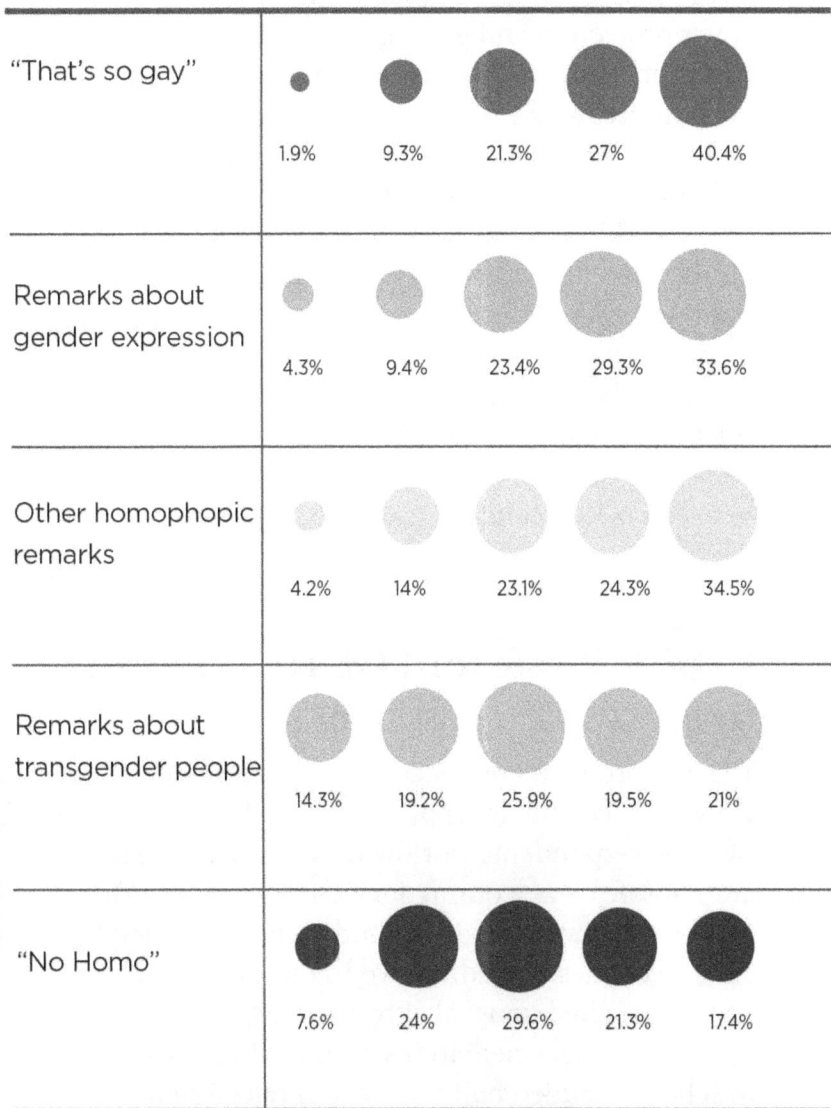

Source: National School Climate Survey, 2015   Graphic by Haley Gable

68 What should inclusive health teachings address?

Lesbian, gay and bisexual health lessons are similar to lessons for straight sexual health. They would cover protection and getting tested often to avoid transmitting sexual diseases. Protection is not just to prevent pregnancy but also to protect against viruses including HIV. According to Womenshealth.gov, lesbians can pass disease through menstrual blood, oral sex, skin-to-skin contact, sex toys and vaginal fluids. Some infections are passed more readily between women than between women and men. A study published by the National Institutes of Health reported that young gay, bisexual and questioning males said sex education rarely addressed their behaviors or risks. Lessons could include sex between males, condom use and transmission of disease.

69 Is it safe for LGBTQ+ students to participate in school sports?

This is a problem area, according to the World Economic Forum. It reported in 2016 that 73 percent of 9,500 respondents worldwide said team sports are not safe or welcoming for LGBTQ+ people. The report, the first such global study, was conducted by six universities, including two in the United States. The report cited unusual agreement across genders, ages and sexual orientations on this. Problems in school included bullying, fear of rejection by

Feeling unsafe

Percentage of LGBTQ students who avoid spaces at the school because they feel unsafe or uncomfortable.

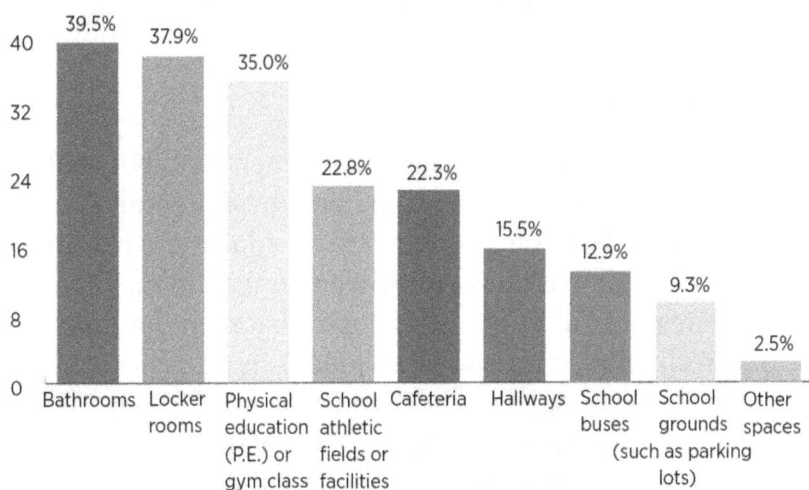

Bathrooms	39.5%
Locker rooms	37.9%
Physical education (P.E.) or gym class	35.0%
School athletic fields or facilities	22.8%
Cafeteria	22.3%
Hallways	15.5%
School buses	12.9%
School grounds (such as parking lots)	9.3%
Other spaces	2.5%

Source: National School Climate Survey, 2015   Graphic by Nicholas Kemp

teammates and discrimination from coaches. Students most frequently encountered homophobia in the stands at games and physical education class. The report is at outonthefields.com

70 Do gay and bisexual people hide their identity at work?

It depends. Sexual orientation and gender identity are not federally protected classifications, so employers can fire people based on sexuality. This means some people conceal their orientations to keep their jobs. Other companies are accepting. They adopt anti-discrimination policies specifically for sexual orientation, even in cases where their states have not.

71 Why are certain occupations stereotyped as masculine or feminine?

Occupational stereotypes occur when a field or skill area is perceived to be dominated by one gender or another. For example, elementary education, nursing and social work have more women than men. The Bureau of Labor Statistics found that men dominated production, craft and labor jobs. This leads people to think of "female jobs" and "male jobs." When someone works in a field typically associated with another gender, their sexual orientation is sometimes questioned. One challenge is that they might be tagged as gay or lesbian for breaking gender norms. This is why some people stereotype male hairdressers as gay and female construction workers as lesbian.

72 Can LGBTQ+ people serve in the U.S. military?

Yes, and they do. LGBTQ+ people serve in the armed forces in many countries. In the U.S. military, they were banned into the 21st century, but President Barack Obama in 2011 repealed the ban on openly gay people serving. The debate today is primarily about transgender people, not gay, lesbian or bisexual people. In March 2018, the Trump administration and the Department of Defense endorsed a plan to limit military service by transgender people and the issue went to the courts.

73 What was the "don't ask, don't tell" policy?

This policy barred people who were openly gay from serving in the U.S. armed forces. The policy allowed the military to discharge individuals who came out. The Clinton administration enacted it in 1994. It was meant to allow gay people to remain in the military but to protect them from being asked about their sexual orientation and prevent them from disclosing it. When President Obama signed the repeal of the policy, he said it had forced gay and lesbian military personnel to lie about their identities and sanctioned closeting.

Religion

74 How do various religions view same-sex marriage?

Positions are changing, and acceptance is generally growing. Perhaps the key indicator of a religion's acceptance is whether it allows same-sex marriage. This is how the Pew Research Center described religions' positions:

Sanction same-sex marriage

- Conservative Jewish Movement
- Episcopal Church
- Evangelical Church in America
- Presbyterian Church (U.S.A.)
- Reform Jewish Movement
- Society of Friends (Quakers)
- Unitarian Universalist Association of Churches
- United Church of Christ

Prohibit same-sex marriage

- American Baptist Churches
- Assemblies of God
- Church of Jesus Christ of Latter-Day Saints (Mormons)
- Islam

- Lutheran Church-Missouri Synod
- National Baptist Convention
- Orthodox Jewish Movement
- Roman Catholic Church
- Southern Baptist Convention
- United Methodist Church

No clear position
- Buddhism
- Hinduism

Same-sex marriage support by religion

Percentage of U.S. adults who favor same-sex marriage, by religion (2001-2017)

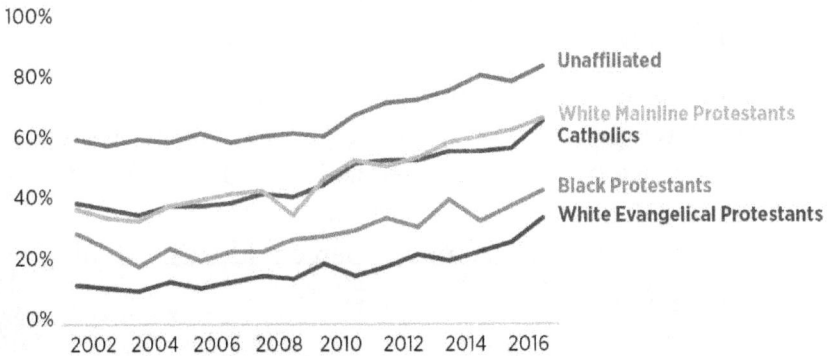

Unaffiliated

White Mainline Protestants
Catholics

Black Protestants
White Evangelical Protestants

100%
80%
60%
40%
20%
0%

2002 2004 2006 2008 2010 2012 2014 2016

Source: Pew Research Center   Graphic by Sherri Days

75 Do people agree with their religion's positions on same-sex marriage?

Often they disagree. Most religions must take a clear yes-or-no position, but followers decide individually. Pew found in 2017 that two-thirds of Catholics and 68 percent of White mainline Protestants supported same-sex marriage. Support among Black Protestants and White Evangelical Protestants remained lower. However, support from White Evangelical Protestants had grown from 27 percent to 35 percent in just one year.

76 How many lesbian, gay and bisexual people identify with a religion?

According to the Pew Research Center, about half of such people are affiliated with an organized religion. Forty-two percent identified as Christian, 2 percent as Jewish and 8 percent as another religion. For the overall population, about 77 percent identified with a religion.

Civil Rights

77 What is marriage equality?

Marriage equality is legal recognition of same-sex marriage. On June 26, 2015, the U.S. Supreme Court ruled in favor of same-sex marriage nationwide. That established marriage equality in the United States. Just one month before the ruling, 72 percent of Americans surveyed had told Pew that legal recognition of same-sex marriage was inevitable. However, national LGBTQ+ protections don't extend to other rights, so social justice work is ongoing.

78 What was the Defense of Marriage Act?

The Clinton administration implemented the Defense of Marriage Act in 1996. It limited marriage to one man and one woman. It said states did not have to recognize same-sex marriages recognized by other states. It also said the federal government was not bound by states' legal recognition of same-sex marriages. In 2013, the U.S. Supreme Court ruled that the government could not discriminate against same-sex married couples in determining federal benefits and protections.

79 Do other countries recognize same-sex marriage?

According to the Pew Research Center, more than 20 countries allow same-sex marriages. The Netherlands became the first in 2000. Others in Europe include Spain, France, Denmark, Sweden, Finland, Norway, Iceland and Ireland. Other countries with legal same-sex marriage are Canada, Argentina, Brazil, Colombia, Uruguay, New Zealand, South Africa and parts of Mexico. In 2017, Taiwan's Constitutional Court ruled that same-sex couples should have the right to marry. Bermuda's Supreme Court legalized same-sex marriage in 2017 and again in 2018 after Parliament replaced it with domestic partnerships.

80 What is the First Amendment Defense Act?

This act was first introduced in Congress in 2015. The bill is designed to protect individuals and corporations who say their beliefs require them to refuse to serve LGBTQ+ individuals. Those beliefs could lead them to deny service based on clients' sexual orientation and gender identity. In 2018, on a 7-2 vote, the U.S. Supreme Court ruled in favor of a Colorado baker who said his Christian convictions prevented him from baking a wedding cake for a same-sex couple. The court ruled that Colorado's civil rights commission had downplayed the baker's religious rights. The ruling was narrowly focused and

How many people know?

Percent saying all or most of the important people in their life are aware that they are LGBT.

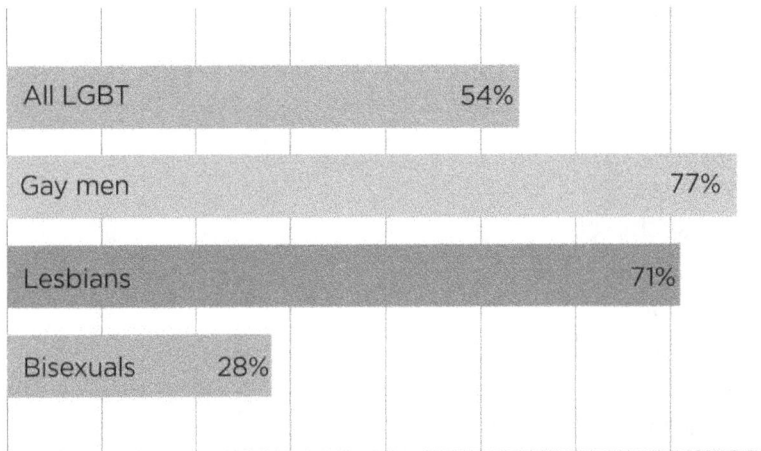

All LGBT	54%
Gay men	77%
Lesbians	71%
Bisexuals	28%

not about the larger issue of whether services may be denied.

81 Do people have protections against being fired for their sexual orientation?

No federal law specifically protects people from being fired or denied a job because of their sexual orientation. However, the Equal Employment Opportunity Commission has stated that sex discrimination law offers such protection. According to the Gill Foundation, the following 20 states, as well as some cities and counties, ensure sexual orientation does not factor into hiring, promotions or termination:

California
Colorado
Connecticut
Delaware
Hawaii
Illinois
Iowa
Maine
Maryland
Massachusetts
Minnesota
Nevada
New Hampshire
New Jersey
New Mexico
New York
Oregon
Rhode Island
Vermont
Washington
Washington, D.C.

82 Can LGBTQ+ people be denied housing based on their sexual orientation?

Seventeen states and some localities have laws preventing housing and job discrimination based on sexual orientation or gender identity. The federal Fair Housing Act prohibits housing and job discrimination based on race, religion, national origin, status or disability. It does not cover sexual orientation or gender identity.

Politics

83 Is the LGBTQ+ movement united or divided?

The diverse groups under the LGBTQ+ umbrella have been expanding their missions and memberships. They appear to be working together more frequently. There are different ideas about how to pursue equality. According to a Pew Research study, half of LGB respondents said they should be able to achieve equality while maintaining a distinct culture. However, others said it is better to achieve equality as part of mainstream culture and institutions.

84 Are LGBTQ+ groups working together more now?

It appears that way. In the past, it seemed sexual orientation initiatives would be jeopardized if paired with rights for gender minorities, which are more controversial. In some cases, provisions for transgender rights were cut out of proposed legislation to win votes for sexual orientation rights. One consequence was that transgender advocates started their own organizations. The two movements now work better together. Some organizations broadened their mission and changed their names to reflect this. Because the groups are now more closely allied, opposition to transgender rights is being treated like earlier opposition to gay rights.

85 Are more anti-LGBTQ+ laws being proposed?

A Movement Advancement Project analysis of public policy counted more than 300 such bills in state houses in 2016 and the first five months of 2017. Ten were approved. Research analyst Alex Sheldon said, "The clear message to LGBT people: You are not welcome." Given the stronger alliance of gay and transgender advocates, these are getting more pushback.

86 Why do some align sexual orientation with economic, political and women's rights?

Supporters from various groups bundle these issues together because they are connected and to build solidarity. When challenges for disadvantaged groups overlap, this is the intersectionality described earlier. It means not just that people can be disadvantaged for more than one reason. It means that the experience can be quite different than for those having just one of the qualities. The issues must be addressed together, not in isolation.

87 How do LGBTQ+ people lean politically?

A 2016 Pew survey found that nearly 90 percent of lesbian, gay and bisexual voters gave Republican presidential nominee Donald Trump a rating of cold on a "feeling thermometer." Sixty-one percent rated Democratic nominee Hillary Clinton warmly. LBGTQ+ voters voted more heavily for Democrats in earlier elections, as well. However, Log Cabin Republicans, a group that is more than 40 years old, has called for greater LGBTQ+ inclusion despite the party's otherwise conservative views.

88 What were sodomy laws?

State laws have used the term to outlaw different sex acts. Some laws banned anal and oral sex and bestiality, which were sometimes grouped together as "unnatural acts" or "crimes against nature." Prior to 1962, sodomy was a felony in every state. By 2002, 36 states had either repealed the laws or courts had overturned them. The next year, anti-sodomy laws were ruled to be unconstitutional. In 2018, Louisiana considered legislation to ban bestiality, treating it separately from acts between consenting adults.

Myths and Stereotypes

89 Are gay, lesbian and bisexual people more affluent than others?

This is complicated because studies find gay and lesbian people who are both richer and poorer than their peer groups. Characteristics such as race and education come into play, too. In 2015, University of Washington professor Marieka Klawitter analyzed 31 studies on this issue. She found that, on average, gay men earned 11 percent less than heterosexual men. Lesbians, on average, earned 9 percent more than heterosexual women. The American Sociological Review highlighted a discrepancy between pay for heterosexuals and bisexuals. On average, bisexual men make 89 cents to each dollar earned by heterosexual men and bisexual women make 93 cents for each dollar earned by straight women. On the high end, the U.S. Census Bureau's 2013 American Communities Survey showed married same-sex couples had an average household income of about $115,000. That compared to $101,487 for married straight couples. The gap was wider for unmarried couples: $111,223 for unmarried same-sex couples compared to $69,511 for unmarried straight couples. The Atlantic magazine wrote in 2014, "like most stereotypes, the myth of gay affluence is greatly exaggerated. … few cultural outlets accurately represent the realities gays and lesbians face in America today." It cited poverty, discrimination, homelessness and food insecurity.

90 Are LGBTQ+ people more likely than others to prey on children?

According to the American Psychological Association, children are not more likely to be molested by LGBTQ+ people. The finding was confirmed by University of California professor Gregory Herek. His review of various studies found no evidence that gay people molest children more than heterosexual people do. The Child Molestation Research & Prevention Institute found that most predators are men married to women.

91 Do people become gay, lesbian or bisexual because of abuse or bad parenting?

Child abuse does not appear to be more prevalent in the upbringing of gay, lesbian or bisexual people, the American Psychiatric Association reported in 2000. Advocates for Youth also has found that sexual abuse is not identifiable as a direct cause for young people being gay. While there is no clear evidence that abuse influences a person's sexual orientation, people do get targeted for abuse if they disclose or are presumed to be LGBTQ+. A study published by the National Institutes of Health reported that "sequencing of maltreatment and emerging sexuality is difficult to ascertain."

92 Do people who are not straight wish they were?

In a 2013 Pew study, 46 percent of gay men and 38 percent of lesbians said their orientation is a positive factor. Twenty-two percent of bisexuals agreed. In all three groups, many said it is neither positive nor negative.

93 Why do some people question whether bisexuality is legitimate?

Bisexuality challenges people's thinking. One way to deal with that is to believe it does not exist. A study presented at the 2013 meeting of the American Public Health Association showed that 15 percent of people were skeptical. They believed bisexual people were confused or transitioning. However, American Institute of Bisexuality President John Sylla said research "completely validates that bisexual people exist." Furthermore, a Williams Institute analysis of national surveys shows that the number of bisexual people is larger than the number who identify as gay or lesbian. However, stigmas including denial among both straight and gay people discourage bi people from disclosing and can make them feel delegitimized.

94 What is bisexual erasure?

Bisexual erasure is when the legitimacy or existence of bisexuality is questioned or denied, according to GLAAD. Also called bisexual invisibility, erasure can contribute to reduced access to resources and support. Erasure can make bisexuals feel like they aren't important or don't exist. Bisexuality Visibility Day, first observed in 1999, was a response to marginalization of bisexual people in both the straight and broader LGBT communities. A study by Dr. Gilbert Gonzales published in the Journal of the American Medical Association reported that, "Bisexual people are not only marginalized by the larger heterosexual population, but also some bisexual individuals may experience stigma from gay and lesbian individuals, resulting in lower connections with the sexual minority community. ... This ostracizing may lead to social isolation, a risk factor for psychological distress."

95 Do bisexual people prefer one gender over others?

Some do, some do not and for some bisexual people, it can change depending on whom they meet. It is natural to ask the question when one is used to thinking in an either/or monosexual frame of mind.

96 Are bisexual people promiscuous?

As is the case with all people, gay or straight, some are and some are not. This stereotype comes from the idea that if someone is attracted to more than one gender, they have more partners. The number of partners someone has depends on many more factors than sexual orientation.

97 Is one's sexual orientation just a phase?

Sexual orientation is part of identity. Just as straight people know they are straight, gay or bi people know that about themselves. For some, sexual orientation is fluid. While social opposition might delay people in accepting their sexual orientation and coming out, it is not a choice.

98 Do certain sports attract more gay or lesbian people than others?

The kind of gender stereotyping that occurs at work also happens in sports. This can create stereotypes about sexual orientation. One cannot assume a person's sexual orientation from what sport they play. Some teams do wind up with more people of one sexual orientation than others, but it is wrong to assume this is always the case. It is also a misjudgment to assume a person's sexual orientation on the basis of what sport they like. As barriers to women have been broken, sports sex stereotypes are falling, too.

99 Are lesbian and gay athletes accepted in sports?

Not always. The 2016 World Economic Forum study of sports globally found that around half of respondents said they had experienced homophobia in sports. Eighty percent reported verbal harassment. Seventy-eight percent said they did not feel it is safe for openly gay people to be spectators at sporting events. Gay-inclusive sports clubs and events have been created to let people compete without harassment.

100 Are drag queens and kings gay?

These are men who perform as women and women who perform as men. They may be straight, gay, bi or transgender, though their acts are about performance art, not about sexual orientation or gender identity.

Timeline

1897: Magnus Hirschfeld establishes the Scientific-Humanitarian Committee in Berlin. It is the world's first gay-rights organization.

1924: Henry Gerber founds the Society for Human Rights in Chicago.

1948: Alfred Kinsey publishes "Sexual Behavior in the Human Male" a psychology paper that argues homosexuality is not a disease.

1950: Harry Hay founds the Mattachine Society in Los Angeles, the first continuing national gay rights organization.

1955: The first lesbian rights organization, Daughters of Bilitis, is founded in San Francisco by Del Martin and Phyllis Lyon.

1957: Frank Kameny, an astronomer in the U.S. Army's Army Map Service, is dismissed for being gay. His protest has been called the spearhead of early militancy for gay rights. In 1961, Kameny and Jack Nichols found the Washington, D.C., chapter of the Mattachine Society. Kameny goes on to organize the Gay Activists Alliance, the National Gay Task Force and the National Gay Rights Lobby.

1962: Illinois becomes the first state to repeal sodomy laws.

1969: Police raid the Stonewall Inn, a bar in New York City's Greenwich Village frequented by LGBTQ+ people. The raid and ensuing riots become a defining moment.

1970: The first Gay Pride march is held in New York City to commemorate the one-year anniversary of the Stonewall riots.

1973: The American Psychiatric Association votes to remove homosexuality from its list of mental illnesses.

1974: Kathy Kozachenko becomes the first out candidate elected to political office in the United States, winning a city council race in Ann Arbor, Michigan.

1977: Harvey Milk becomes the first openly gay person elected to public office in California, winning office as a San Francisco city-county supervisor. The next year, Milk and Mayor George Moscone are assassinated in City Hall.

1981: In June, the HIV/AIDS epidemic breaks out in the United States.

1982: Wisconsin becomes the first state to outlaw discrimination against gay people.

1987: The March on Washington demands President Ronald Reagan address the AIDS epidemic. He does not publicly acknowledge it until the end of his presidency in 1989.

1990: President George H.W. Bush signs the Ryan White Care Act, which provides federal funding for people with AIDS.

1991: National Basketball Association star Magic Johnson announces he is HIV-positive. Johnson, who is heterosexual, becomes an advocate for safe sex and treatment.

1994: The "Don't ask, don't tell" policy signed by President Bill Clinton prohibits discrimination against closeted LGB people in the military but forbids openly LGB people from enlisting.

1996: Clinton signs the Defense of Marriage Act, limiting marriage to one man and one woman at the federal level. It allows states to refuse to recognize same-sex marriage.

2000: Vermont becomes the first state to legalize civil unions between partners of the same sex.

2003: Lawrence v. Texas results in a Supreme Court ruling that sodomy laws are unconstitutional.

2004: Massachusetts becomes the first state to legalize same-sex marriage. By 2010 New Hampshire, Vermont, Connecticut, Iowa and Washington follow.

2004: In the face of sexual harassment accusations, New Jersey Gov. James McGreevey announces he is gay and resigns.

2008: The California Legislature legalizes same-sex marriage in May. Voters amend the state constitution in November to ban it. The ban is overturned in 2013.

2009: President Barack Obama signs The Matthew Shepard and James Byrd Jr. Hate Crimes Prevention Act into law. Shepard was a gay student at the University of Wyoming who was attacked and later died from the injuries. Byrd was an African-American man killed by three White supremacists. The law extends federal hate crime law to cover crimes motivated by a victim's actual or perceived gender, sexual orientation, gender identity or disability.

2011: "Don't ask, don't tell" is repealed.

2011: Obama announces he will not support the Defense of Marriage Act. New York legalizes same-sex marriage.

2015: On June 26, the U.S. Supreme Court legalizes same-sex marriage in all 50 states.

2018: The U.S. Supreme Court votes 7-2 that it was legal for a cake decorator to decline to design a wedding cake for a same-sex couple. The ruling is narrow, stating that the Colorado Civil Rights Commission's actions in assessing the man's religious objections violated the free exercise clause.

Resources

Books & Articles

Archambeau, Kathleen. *Pride & Joy: LGBTQ Artists, Icons and Everyday Heroes.* Coral Gables: Mango. 2017.

Baldwin, James. *Giovanni's Room.* New York: Vintage reprint of 1956 novel. 2013.

Beeching, Vicky. *Undivided: Coming Out, Becoming Whole, and Living Free from Shame.* New York: HarperOne. 2018.

Bronski, Michael. *You Can Tell Just by Looking: And 20 Other Myths about LGBT Life and People.* Boston: Beacon Press. 2013.

Dawson, June. *This Book is Gay.* Naperville: Sourcebooks Fire. 2015.

Downs, Alan. *The Velvet Rage: Overcoming the Pain of Growing Up Gay in a Straight Man's World.* Boston: Da Capo Lifelong Books, revised and updated. 2012.

Eriksen, Telaina. *Unconditional: A Guide to Loving and Supporting Your LGBTQ Child.* Coral Gables: Mango. 2017.

González, Rigoberto. *Butterfly Boy: Memories of a Chicano Mariposa.* Madison: University of Wisconsin Press. 2011.

Gushee, David P. *Changing Our Mind: Definitive 3rd Edition of the Landmark Call for Inclusion of LGBTQ*

Christians with Response to Critics. Canton: Read The Spirit Books. 2017.

Jennings, Kevin. *Always My Child: A Parent's Guide to Understanding Your Gay, Lesbian, Bisexual, Transgendered or Questioning Son or Daughter.* New York: Touchstone. 2003.

Ka'ahumanu, Lani and Loraine Hutchins. *Bi Any Other Name — Bisexual People Speak Out.* New York: Riverdale Avenue Books. 2015.

Lorde, Geraldine Audre. *Zami: A New Spelling of My Name.* Hoboken: Crossing Press. 2011.

Mardell, Ashley. *The ABC's of LGBT+.* Coral Gables: Mango. 2016.

Owens-Reid, Danielle. *This Is a Book for Parents of Gay Kids: A Question & Answer Guide to Everyday Life.* San Francisco: Chronicle Books. 2014.

Riggle, Ellen D.B. and Sharon S. Rostosky. *A Positive View of LGBTQ: Embracing Identity and Cultivating Well-Being.* New York: Rowman & Littlefield Publishers reprint. 2011.

Rosswood, Eric. *The Ultimate Guide for Gay Dads: Everything You Need to Know About LGBTQ Parenting but are (Mostly) Afraid to Ask.* Coral Gables: Mango. 2017.

Rupp, Leila J. and Susan Freeman (eds.) *Understanding and Teaching U.S. Lesbian, Gay, Bisexual and Transgender History.* Madison: University of Wisconsin Press. 2014.

Savage, Dan and Terry Miller. *It Gets Better: Coming Out, Overcoming Bullying, and Creating a Life Worth Living.* New York: Penguin Books reprint. 2012.

Sue, Derald Wing. *Microaggressions in Everyday Life: Race, Gender, and Sexual Orientation*. Hoboken: Wiley. 2010.

Zakar, Michael and Zach Zakar. *Pray the Gay Away*. Zakar Twins. 2017.

pbs.org/wgbh/americanexperience/features/timeline/stonewall/

Organizations

AIDS United, aidsunited.org

American Association for Marriage and Family Therapy, aamft.org

American Civil Liberties Union's Lesbian Gay Bisexual Transgender Project, aclu.org/lgbt

American Foundation for AIDS Research, amfar.org

American Institute of Bisexuality, bisexual.org

American Psychological Association, apa.org/pi/lgbt

Asexuality Visibility and Education Network, www.facebook.com/AVENOfficial/

BiNet USA, binetusa.org

Bisexual Resource Center, biresource.org

Black AIDS Institute, blackaids.org

Campus Pride, campuspride.org

The Community of LGBT Centers, lgbtcenters.org

Community United Against Violence, cuav.org

The Elizabeth Taylor AIDS Foundation, elizabethtayloraidsfoundation.org

Equality Michigan Action Network, equalitymiaction. org/

Family Acceptance Project, familyproject.sfsu.edu

Gay & Lesbian Advocates & Defenders, glad.org

Gay and Lesbian Medical Association, glma.org

Gay-Straight Alliance Network, gsanetwork.org

Gill Foundation, gillfoundation.org

GLAAD, glaad.org

GLSEN (Gay, Lesbian and Straight Education Network), glsen.org

GMHC (Gay Men's Health Crisis), gmhc.org

Human Rights Campaign, hrc.org

Human Rights Watch Lesbian, Gay, Bisexual, and Transgender Rights Program, hrw.org/lgbt

Lambda Legal Defense and Education Fund, lambdalegal.org

League of United Latin American Citizens (LULAC) LGBT Program, lulac.org/programs/lgbt

Matthew Shepard Foundation, matthewshepard.org

The Movement Advancement Project, lgbtmap.org

The Naming Project, thenamingproject.org

National Black Justice Coalition, nbjc.org

National Center for Lesbian Rights, nclrights.org

National Gay and Lesbian Task Force, thetaskforce.org

National Lesbian & Gay Journalists Association, nlgja. org

National LGBT Health Education Center, lgbthealtheducation.org

Network on Religion & Justice for Asian and Pacific Islander LGBT People, netrj.org

PFLAG (Parents, Families and Friends of Lesbians and Gays), pflag.org

The Pride Network, thepridenetwork.org

Pride Source, producesource.com

The Trevor Project, thetrevorproject.org

Triangle Foundation, equalitymi.org

Williams Institute, UCLA School of Law, williamsinstitute.law.ucla.edu

Epilogue

The Bias Busters series helps people have better conversations across lines where misunderstanding and stereotyping often occur. The step beyond understanding is to become an ally. There is a long tradition of people being allies for the gay community and it can happen in our families, at work, school or in our communities. One of the largest organizations for allies is PFLAG (Parents, Families and Friends of Lesbians and Gays). Founded in 1972, PFLAG has more than 400 local chapters and a wealth of resources online, including a guide on being a good ally.

Allies can be a powerful force for change and strong supporters for lesbian, gay and bisexual people. We hope this guide can be a first step, leading to deeper conversations with more people and, as Horowitz and Gushee write at the beginning of the guide, actions. People will tell you what kind of support they appreciate from allies. It is probably not speaking for them, as they can speak for themselves. One expression for this is to step back and let others step forward so they may speak for themselves. Allies can do a lot by listening to people, supporting them and standing with them as they work for greater visibility, acceptance and freedom.

Whether you decide to be an ally or not, we hope you have conversations about experiences, obstacles and aspirations. You're likely to find that people are not as different from each other as they first think.

Discussion and Reflection

This guide, like all the guides in our series, is intended as just a starting point. We hope that these 100 questions and answers will be just a first step toward deeper understanding. These are some questions for small-group discussions or personal reflection. They are written for straight people, but can be for everyone. Having lesbian, gay and bisexual people in a discussion group can help, of course.

- How have you noticed someone's acceptance of lesbian, gay and bisexual people in general changes after they learn about a friend or relative's orientation?
- What can a bystander say when someone jokes about gay people or uses expressions like "that's so gay," or says someone is "a queer?"
- Military policy used to be "don't ask, don't tell." What are the implications for acceptance and living authentically if we are not allowed to discuss something important about ourselves?

- In what everyday ways can straight people support lesbian, gay and bisexual people?
- Consider the difference between tolerance and acceptance. Where are you on that scale?
- What would you say to someone who trusted you enough to come out to you?
- What could you do to help one member of your family accept that another member was lesbian, gay or bisexual? Contrast the situation for different relatives.
- If, after years of friendship, someone revealed they were lesbian, gay or bisexual, how would that affect your friendship? Would it depend on which orientation they expressed?
- Think about an awkward exchange you have had with a person who is lesbian, gay or bi. What would you do in the same situation now to make that less awkward?
- Stereotypes can come in bunches. What stereotypes are applied to lesbian, gay and bisexual people. Why?
- Acceptance of people has increased, especially among younger generations, but equality still has not been achieved. What privileges do straight people have, such as being treated as "normal," or not being judged for holding hands in public, that lesbian, gay and bisexual people don't have?

Next Steps

The Pew Research center says that about nine Americans in 10 know someone who is gay. But how well do we know them? Have coffee or lunch with an LGBTQ+ acquaintance, not to discuss their sexual orientation, but to get to know them better as a person.

Alternatively, if you are already close to someone who is LGBTQ+, ask them to share the challenges they regularly face from others. You might be surprised.

PFLAG and other organizations welcome people who want to support LGBTQ+ family members and friends. Join one of their meetings.

All kinds of groups have public events every year. Groups for LGBTQ+ people do, too, and can use lots of help from allies. Volunteer to help with an event.

Controversies can arise at the juncture of faith and sexuality. Many groups, including faith-based ones, hold discussions on this issue. You don't have to be LGBTQ+ or related to someone who is or even be a member of the faith to join the discussion. Go hear what people are talking about, listening for different points of view.

Our Story

The 100 Questions and Answers series springs from the idea that good journalism should increase cross-cultural competence and understanding. Most of our guides are created by Michigan State University journalism students.

We use journalistic interviews to surface the simple, everyday questions that people have about each other but might be afraid to ask. We use research and reporting to get the answers and then put them where people can find them, read them and learn about each other.

These cultural competence guides are meant to be conversation starters. We want people to use these guides to get some baseline understanding and to feel comfortable asking more questions. We put a resources section in every guide we make and we arrange community conversations. While the guides can answer questions in private, they are meant to spark discussions.

Making these has taught us that people are not that different from each other. People share more similarities than differences. We all want the same things for ourselves and for our families. We want to be accepted, respected and understood.

Please email your thoughts and suggestions to Series Editor Joe Grimm at joe.grimm@gmail.com, at the Michigan State University School of Journalism.

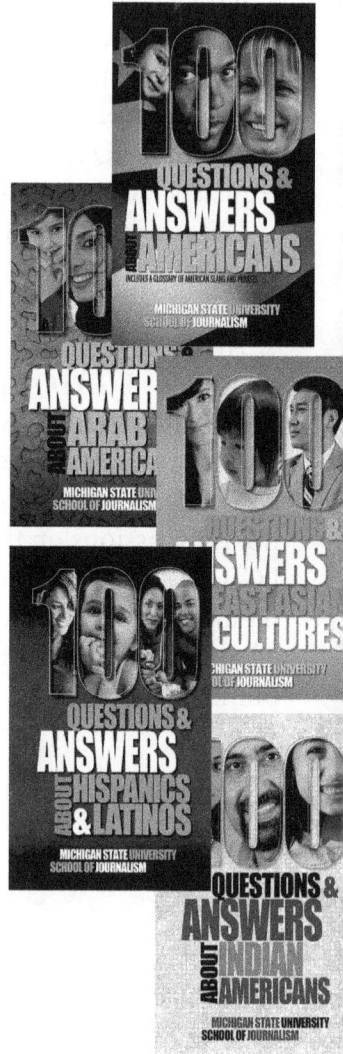

http://news.jrn.msu.edu/culturalcompetence

Companion Guide

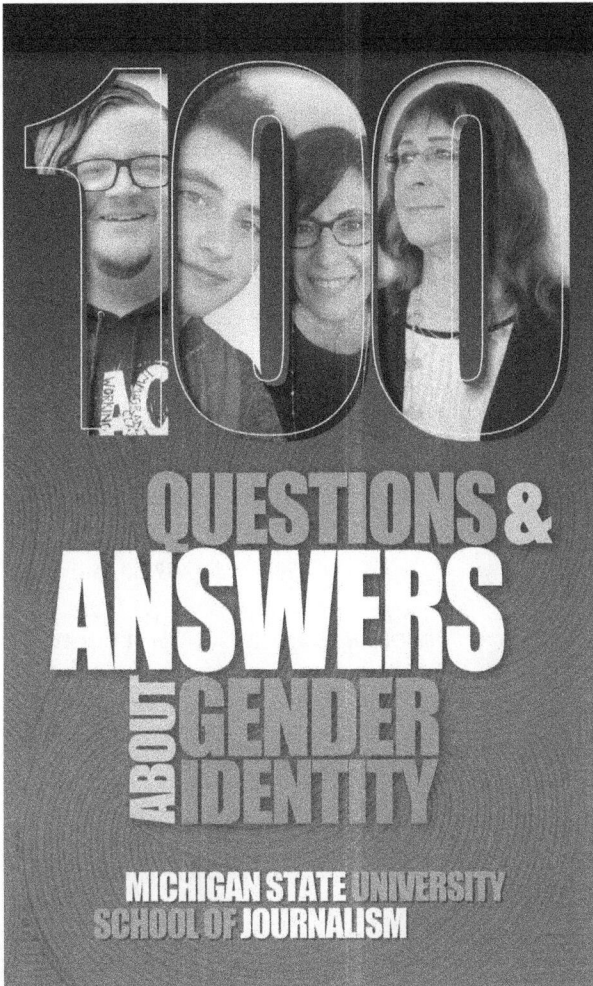

Read the companion guide to *100 Questions and Answers About Sexual Orientation*. This simple, introductory guide answers 100 of the basic questions people ask about transgender people in everyday conversation. The questions come from interviews with transgender people who say these are issues they frequently get asked about or wish people knew more about.

ISBN: 978-1-64180-002-0

Related Books

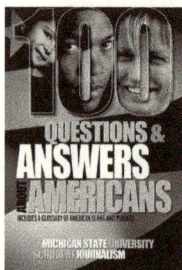

100 Questions and Answers About Americans
Michigan State University School of Journalism, 2013
This guide answers some of the first questions asked by newcomers to the United States. Questions represent dozens of nationalities coming from Africa, Asia, Australia, Europe and North and South America. Good for international students, guests and new immigrants.
http://news.jrn.msu.edu/culturalcompetence/

ISBN: 978-1-939880-20-8

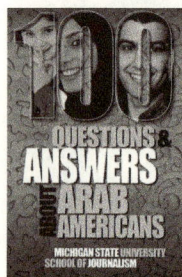

100 Questions and Answers About Arab Americans
Michigan State University School of Journalism, 2014
The terror attacks of Sept. 11, 2001, propelled these Americans into a difficult position where they are victimized twice. The guide addresses stereotypes, bias and misinformation. Key subjects are origins, religion, language and customs. A map shows places of national origin.
http://news.jrn.msu.edu/culturalcompetence/

ISBN: 978-1-939880-56-7

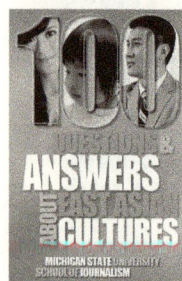

100 Questions and Answers About East Asian Cultures
Michigan State University School of Journalism, 2014
Large university enrollments from Asia prompted this guide as an aid for understanding cultural differences. The focus is on people from China, Japan, Korea and Taiwan and includes Mongolia, Hong Kong and Macau. The guide includes history, language, values, religion, foods and more.
http://news.jrn.msu.edu/culturalcompetence/

ISBN: 978-939880-50-5

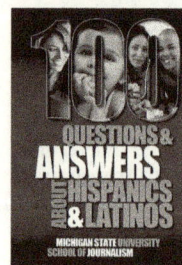

100 Questions and Answers About Hispanics & Latinos
Michigan State University School of Journalism, 2014
This group became the largest ethnic minority in the United States in 2014 and this guide answers many of the basic questions about it. Questions were suggested by Hispanics and Latinos. Includes maps and charts on origin and size of various Hispanic populations.
http://news.jrn.msu.edu/culturalcompetence/

ISBN: 978-1-939880-44-4

Print and ebooks available on Amazon.com and other retailers.

Related Books

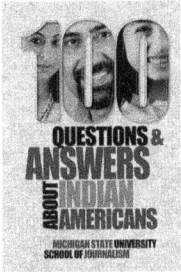

100 Questions and Answers About Indian Americans
Michigan State University School of Journalism, 2013
In answering questions about Indian Americans, this guide also addresses Pakistanis, Bangladeshis and others from South Asia. The guide covers religion, issues of history, colonization and national partitioning, offshoring and immigration, income, education, language and family.
http://news.jrn.msu.edu/culturalcompetence/

ISBN: 978-1-939880-00-0 m

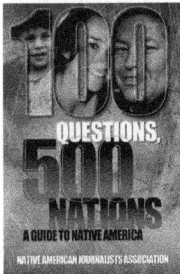

100 Questions, 500 Nations: A Guide to Native America
Michigan State University School of Journalism, 2014
This guide was created in partnership with the Native American Journalists Association. The guide covers tribal sovereignty, treaties and gaming, in addition to answers about population, religion, U.S. policies and politics. The guide includes the list of federally recognized tribes.
http://news.jrn.msu.edu/culturalcompetence/

ISBN: 978-1-939880-38-3

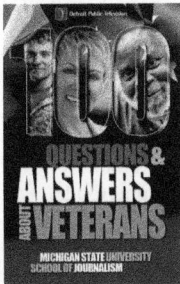

100 Questions and Answers About Veterans
Michigan State University School of Journalism, 2015
This guide treats the more than 20 million U.S. military veterans as a cultural group with distinctive training, experiences and jargon. Graphics depict attitudes, adjustment challenges, rank, income and demographics. Includes six video interviews by Detroit Public Television.
http://news.jrn.msu.edu/culturalcompetence/

ISBN: 978-1-942011-00-2

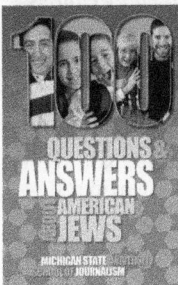

100 Questions and Answers About American Jews
Michigan State University School of Journalism 2016
We begin by asking and answering what it means to be Jewish in America. The answers to these wide-ranging, base-level questions will ground most people and set them up for meaningful conversations with Jewish acquaintances.
http://news.jrn.msu.edu/culturalcompetence/

ISBN: 978-1-942011-22-4

Print and ebooks available on Amazon.com and other retailers.

Related Books

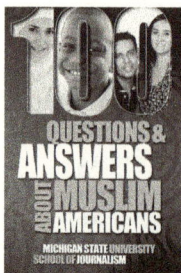

100 Questions and Answers About Muslim Americans
Michigan State University School of Journalism, 2014
This guide was done at a time of rising intolerance in the United States toward Muslims. The guide describes the presence of this religious group around the world and inside the United States. It includes audio on how to pronounce some basic Muslim words.
http://news.jrn.msu.edu/culturalcompetence/

ISBN: 978-1-939880-79-6

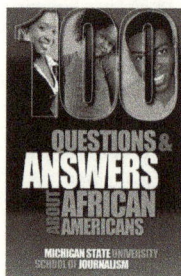

100 Questions and Answers About African Americans
Michigan State University School of Journalism, 2016
Learn about the racial issues that W.E.B. DuBois said in 1900 would be the big challenge for the 20th century. This guide explores Black and African American identity, history, language, contributions and more. Learn more about current issues in American cities and campuses.
http://news.jrn.msu.edu/culturalcompetence/

ISBN: 978-1-942011-19-4

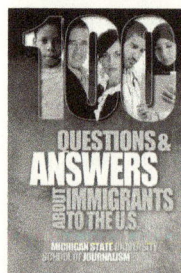

100 Questions and Answers About Immigrants to the U.S.
Michigan State University School of Journalism 2016
This simple, introductory guide answers 100 of the basic questions people ask about U.S. immigrants and immigration in everyday conversation. It has answers about identity, language, religion, culture, customs, social norms, economics, politics, education, work, families and food.

ISBN: 978-1-934879-63-4

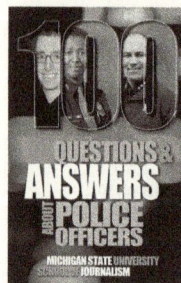

100 Questions and Answers about Police Officers
Michigan State University School of Journalism 2018
This simple, introductory guide answers 100 of the basic questions people ask about police officers, sheriff's deputies, public safety officers and tribal police. It focuses on policing at the local level, where procedures vary from coast to coast. The guide includes a resource about traffic stops.

ISBN: 978-1-64180-013-6

Print and ebooks available on Amazon.com and other retailers.